WORLD CHAMPION TEACHES YOU TO PLAY TABLE TENNIS

世界冠军教你打乒乓球

（汉英双语）

刘伟　姚卫　编著
Liu Wei　Yao Wei

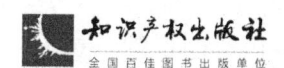

图书在版编目（CIP）数据

世界冠军教你打乒乓球：汉、英 / 刘伟，姚卫编著. —北京：知识产权出版社，2018.11
ISBN 978-7-5130-5912-1

Ⅰ. ①世… Ⅱ. ①刘… ②姚… Ⅲ. ①乒乓球运动—基本知识—汉、英 Ⅳ. ① G846

中国版本图书馆 CIP 数据核字 (2018) 第 236513 号

内容提要

本书为汉英双语图书，对乒乓球运动的基础知识及各种基本技法要领进行了详细的说明，对近几年出现的新技术作了精确阐述，并配有相应的技术动作分解图。本书还有配套的动作示范视频，汉英双语解说，适合中外乒乓球爱好者学习使用。

责任编辑：田　姝　　　　　　　　　责任印制：刘译文

世界冠军教你打乒乓球
SHIJIE GUANJUN JIAO NI DA PINGPANGQIU

刘伟　姚卫　编著

出版发行	知识产权出版社 有限责任公司	网　　址	http://www.ipph.cn
电　　话	010-82004826		http://www.laichushu.com
社　　址	北京市海淀区气象路50号院	邮　　编	100081
责编电话	010-82000860转8598	责编邮箱	tianshu@cnipr.com
发行电话	010-82000860转8101	发行传真	010-82000893
印　　刷	北京中献拓方科技发展有限公司	经　　销	各大网上书店、新华书店及相关书店
开　　本	720mm×1000mm　1/16	印　　张	12.75
版　　次	2018年11月第1版	印　　次	2018年11月第1次印刷
字　　数	300千字	定　　价	68.00元

ISBN 978-7-5130-5912-1

出版权专有　侵权必究
如有印装质量问题，本社负责调换。

前　言

乒乓球运动于19世纪后期起源于英国，流行于欧洲。它是由网球运动派生而来的。在20世纪50年代，中国的乒乓球运动得到了飞速发展。在全国范围内开展了群众性乒乓球运动，使乒乓球技术水平得到了很大提高。1959年中国优秀运动员容国团第一次夺得世界乒乓球锦标赛的男子单打冠军，标志着中国乒乓球运动在世界的崛起。1961年中国主办了第26届世界乒乓球锦标赛。在这届比赛中中国运动员力争上游，一举夺取了3项冠军，包括争夺最激烈的男子团体冠军奖杯——思韦斯林杯。从此，中国乒乓球运动走到了世界前列。在20世纪80年代的5届世乒赛中，中国运动员获得了金牌总数的80%。此后，乒乓球就成为中国的国球，中国运动员始终站在世界乒坛的最顶峰。

当今世界乒乓球运动的发展不太平衡，强盛的中国乒乓球队常常包揽各个项目的冠军。各类比赛的奖牌也主要集中在欧亚地区，不平衡的趋势仍在逐渐加大。为了推进乒乓球运动在世界范围内的普及和提高，促使乒乓球运动健康有序地发展，有必要帮助其他国家地区的运动员及青少年爱好者以科学的方法和先进的技术进行训练，使更多的人能够参与到这项运动中来，使世界乒乓球运动更加繁荣。

本书就是本着把中国乒乓球先进的技术推广到世界，让全世界的乒乓球爱好者共享的目的而撰写。

Foreword

The sport of table tennis originated in Victorian England in the late 19th century and was prevalent in Europe. It was derived from tennis. In the 1950s the sport of table tennis in China developed rapidly. It was carried out as the mass sport across the country so that the technical level of table tennis was greatly improved. In 1959 the Chinese excellent athlete Rong Guotuan won the world table tennis championship of men's single for the first time, which marked the rise of Chinese table tennis in the world. In 1961, China hosted the 26th world table tennis championships. Chinese athletes raced to the top in the contest, winning the three champions at a stroke, including the men's team championship trophy, Swaythling Cup, which was the most intense competition. From then on, the sport of table tennis in China has walked to the front of the world. In the 1980s, Chinese athletes won 80% number of the total gold medals in the five times World Table Tennis Championships. Since then, table tennis has become the national sport of China; the Chinese athletes are always standing on the highest peak in the world table tennis.

In today's world, the development of table tennis is not very balanced; the strong Chinese table tennis team often sweeps the champion of each item. All kinds of medals are also mainly concentrated in Eurasian area. This unbalanced trend is still increasing gradually. In order to promote the popularization and improvement of table tennis in the world, and to accelerate the healthy and orderly development of table tennis, it is necessary to help the athletes and young lovers in other countries and regions with scientific methods and advanced technique training and enable more people to participate in the sport, making a prosperous development of the world table tennis.

The book is written in line with the purpose that is to promote the advanced technique of our national sport to the world, and enable table tennis enthusiasts in the world to share it with us.

目 录

第一章 乒乓球运动的场地与器材 ……………………………1

第一节 乒乓球器材……………………………………………2
第二节 球拍的选择、粘贴与保养……………………………9

第二章 乒乓球基础知识 …………………………………… 15

第一节 基本姿势与站位 …………………………………… 16
第二节 击球路线、时间、部位与拍面角度 ……………… 18

第三章 乒乓球的基本技术 ………………………………… 25

第一节 握拍法 ……………………………………………… 26
第二节 基本步法 …………………………………………… 28
第三节 过渡技术 …………………………………………… 35
第四节 发球技术 …………………………………………… 54
第五节 接发球技术 ………………………………………… 71
第六节 攻球技术 …………………………………………… 75
第七节 弧圈球技术 ………………………………………… 84
第八节 防守性技术 ………………………………………… 96

第四章 乒乓球的基本战术与运用 ………………………… 113

第一节 乒乓球基本战术 …………………………………… 114

第二节　战术的运用 …………………………………………… 136

第五章　乒乓球运动的双打技术 ……………………………… 145
第一节　双打的规则与配对 …………………………………… 146
第二节　双打的站位、步伐与战术 …………………………… 148

第六章　乒乓球运动的比赛知识 ……………………………… 163
第一节　乒乓球竞赛规则简介 ………………………………… 164
第二节　乒乓球裁判法简介 …………………………………… 172
第三节　乒乓球比赛及类型简介 ……………………………… 178
第四节　乒乓球运动竞赛方法 ………………………………… 183

附　录 …………………………………………………………… 193

Contents

Chapter 1 Venue and equipment for table tennis 1

Section 1 Table tennis equipment 2
Section 2 Choosing, gluing and maintenance of rackets 9

Chapter 2 Fundamental knowledge of table tennis 15

Section 1 Ready position and basic stance 16
Section 2 Paths and time of hitting the ball, hitting spot on the ball and angle of racket face 18

Chapter 3 Basic techniques of table tennis 25

Section 1 Ways to grip a racket 26
Section 2 Basic footwork 28
Section 3 Transitional techniques 35
Section 4 Serve techniques 54
Section 5 Receiving techniques 71
Section 6 Attacking techniques 75
Section 7 Loop drive techniques 84
Section 8 Defensive techniques 96

Chapter 4 Basic tactics of table tennis and the application 113

Section 1 Basic tactics of table tennis 114
Section 2 Application of tactics 136

Chapter 5 Doubles techniques of table tennis 145

Section 1 Rules and pairing of doubles 146
Section 2 Formation, footwork and tactics of doubles 148

Chapter 6 Knowledge of table tennis game 163

Section 1 Introduction to the rules of table tennis game 164
Section 2 Brief introduction to the referee law of table tennis 172
Section 3 Brief introduction to the table tennis match and its types 178
Section 4 Competition methods of table tennis 183

Appendix 193

第一章
乒乓球运动的场地与器材

Chapter 1
Venue and equipment for table tennis

第一节
乒乓球器材

Section 1
Table tennis equipment

乒乓球运动具有很强的观赏性和艺术性，对器材有一定的要求。良好的器材是运动参与者发挥较高水平的必要保障

Table tennis has a strong ornamental value and artistic quality; therefore, there are certain requirements for the equipment. Good equipment is the necessary guarantee for the participants of the sport to give full play to a higher level.

1．场地

赛区空间应不小于14米长、7米宽、5米高，四周用不超过1.5米的挡板围起来。

1. Venue

The space of the playing area should not be less than 14 m long, 7 m wide, 5 m high, surrounded by baffles of no more than 1.5 meters high.

2．乒乓球台

乒乓球台台面应由坚实木料制成，具有一定弹性，上层表面叫作比赛台面，长274厘米，宽152.5厘米，无光泽，台边各有2厘米宽的白线，长的称边线，短的称端线。台面中央有一条0.3厘米宽的白线，称为中线，将球台划分为两个相等的"半区"（如图1-1）。

2. Table tennis table

The table-board of table tennis tables should be made of solid wood with certain elasticity; the upper surface is called the playing surface that is 274 cm long, 152.5 cm wide, 76 cm high from the ground and uniformly dark colored with a matte finish. Each edge of the table has a white line of 2 cm wide; the long lines are called side lines, and the short ones are called end lines. A white line of 3 mm wide is in the center of the table-board that is called as the center line, by which the playing surface is divided into two equal "half courts". (As shown in fig.1-1):

图 1-1 乒乓球球台
Fig.1-1 Table tannis table

3. 球网装置

球网装置包括：网、悬网绳、网柱及将它们固定在球台上的夹钳部分。球网的高度为 15.25 厘米，它将台面分成两个大小相等的部分。网垂直于台面，与端线平行，紧贴着网柱和台面。国际比赛规定球网应柔软、呈暗绿色，网柱应与网颜色相同，表面无光泽。（如图 1-2）

3. Net assembly

The net assembly includes: the net、the net hanging twine、the poles and the clamp parts by which the poles are fixed on the table.The net is 15.25 cm high, and it divides the table into two equal parts. The net is perpendicular to the table, parallel with the end lines and close to the net poles and the table surface. The international competition rules stipulate that the net should be soft, dark green, and the net poles should be the same color with a matte surface. (As shown in fig.1-2)

4. 球

国际乒联规定乒乓球的直径 40^+ 毫米，即 40.00 ~ 40.60 毫米；重 2.7 克，呈白色，且无光泽。（如图 1-3）

4. Ball

The International Table Tennis Federation (ITTF) rules specify that the table tennis ball should be colored white with a matte finish and a diameter of 40^+ mm, namely 40.00~40.60 mm, and a mass of 2.7 grams. (As shown in fig.1-3)

图 1-2 乒乓球台球网装置
Fig.1-2 Net assembly

图 1-3 乒乓球
Fig.1-3 Table tennis balls

5. 球拍

根据不同的握法，球拍主要分为横拍与直拍两种，手柄与板面的形状也有所不同。

横板：使用横拍稳定性强，正反手均衡，中远台实力强。（如图1-4）

直板：使用直拍手腕灵活，前三板占优势，反手较弱。（如图1-5）

图1-4 横板

图1-5 直板

球拍两面无论是否有胶皮，都必须无光泽，且一面为鲜红色，另一面为黑色。球拍使用的胶皮应为国际乒联许可的品牌和型号。

6. 胶皮

胶皮是一种粘在乒乓球拍板面上的胶，现在通常所说的胶皮并不是直接粘在板面上的，而是覆盖于海绵上面，胶皮和海绵统称为套胶。

5. Racket

According to different grips table tennis rackets are mainly divided into two kinds: the shake-hand grip racket and the pen-hold grip racket, their handles and surface shapes are also different.

The shake-hand grip racket: playing with the shake-hand grip racket has a strong stability and a balanced force of the forehand and backhand, with a strong force at middle court and back court. (As shown in fig.1-4)

The pen-hold grip racket: playing with the pen-hold grip racket allows the wrist to move flexibly and it is dominant in the first three hits, but backhand is weaker. (As shown in fig.1-5)

Fig.1-4　The shake-hand grip racket

Fig.1-5　The pen-hold grip racket

Both sides of a racket must have a matte finish whether there are rubbers on them or not; and one side must be red while the other side must be black. The rubber sheets used on rackets should be the brands and models licensed by the International Table Tennis Federation.

6. Rubber sheet

Rubber sheet is a kind of rubber glued on the blade of table tennis racket, now known as rubber, which is not glued directly on the surface of the blade but on a piece of sponge, the rubber and the sponge are collectively called as sandwich rubber.

（1）反胶胶皮。

反胶胶皮是由一层海绵上粘贴一块带颗粒的胶皮组成。颗粒朝内，表面光滑（如图1-6）。其特点是击球旋转力强、击球稳定、易控制。反胶胶皮球拍击球稳定，控制球好，因此是初学者首选的类型。粘贴反胶海绵的球拍是目前最流行的，它最大的特点是较好地将旋转和速度结合在一起，在中远台的相持中，回击的稳定性比粘贴其他胶皮的球拍强。

(1) Inverted rubber.

It consists of a sheet of pips out rubber on top of a layer of sponge. The pips point inward, so the surface is smooth. (As shown in fig.1-6) The characteristics: it can make spinning with a strong force and hitting with good stability, also it is easy to control. Because of a stable hitting and good controlling of the ball, therefore, the type is preferred for beginners. At present the rackets glued with inverted rubbers are the most popular. Its greatest feature is a better combination of rotation and speed, and at the stage locked in a stalemate the stability of its return from the middle and back court is better than that of rackets glued with other rubbers.

图 1-6　反胶胶皮

Fig.1-6　Inverted rubber

（2）正胶胶皮。

正胶颗粒的高度应为0.9～1毫米之间（如图1-7）。正胶胶皮球拍的特点是击球的稳定性较好，反弹力较强，回球速度快。直拍近台左推右攻或两面攻的运动员大多喜欢用正胶胶

(2) Pips-out rubber.

It consists of a sheet of pips-out rubber on top of a layer of sponge. The height of the pimples of a pips-out rubber should be between 0.9～1 mm.(As shown in fig.1-7) The characteristics: it hits the ball with fairly good stability and a strong rebound, and returns with fast speed. The most penhold grip athletes in the style of backhand

皮球拍。但它的摩擦力远不如反胶，不能制造强烈的旋转，同时不利于相持阶段中远台技术的发挥。

block with forehand attack or two-winged attack from short court like to use it. But its friction force is much less than that of inverted rubber, and it can't make strong spin, at the same time, it's not conducive to give play to the techniques from the middle and back court at the stage locked in a stalemate.

图 1-7　正胶胶皮

Fig.1-7　Pips-out rubber

（3）生胶胶皮。

生胶胶皮（如图 1-8）与正胶胶皮相似，但生胶胶皮颗粒的直径大于高度，胶体的含胶量比正胶胶皮大，比正胶的胶质更软，弹性更强。其特点是击球下沉，回球速度快，搓球旋转弱。由于生胶有减转的作用，因此特别容易控制球。

(3) Pips-out natural rubber.

The pips-out natural rubber (As shown in fig.1-8) is similar to pips-out rubber, but the diameter of its pimples is greater than the height of the pimples. It just has a bigger colloidal gel content, softer colloid and stronger elasticity than that of pips-out rubber. The characteristics: it hits the ball with a down force and returns with fast speed, but it pushes the ball with weaker spin. Due to the function of reducing spin, therefore the pips-out natural rubber is particularly easy to control.

图 1-8 生胶胶皮
Fig.1-8 Pips-out natural rubber

（4）长胶胶皮。

长胶胶皮（如图1-9）颗粒的直径与高度的比应为1:1.1，颗粒的高度一般在1.6毫米左右。使用这种胶皮一般都加一层1毫米以内的薄海绵，也可以不加海绵。由于长胶的颗粒比较细长，在击球时会出现反旋转现象。即：在回击对方的强烈上旋球或大力扣球时，回球呈下旋；回击对方的不转球时，回球也不转；回击对方下旋球时，回球呈上旋。对方的旋转越强，回球的反旋转也越强。长胶本身不制造较强的旋转，主要是依靠来球的不同旋转而产生相反的旋转。这些反常的变化会造成对方失误或出高球，给自己创造进攻的机会。

(4) Long pips rubber.

The diameter to height ratio of its pimples should be 1 : 1.1; generally, the height of pimples is about 1.6 mm. (As shown in fig.1-9) When using this kind of rubber, usually a layer of thin sponge within 1 mm should be added beneath it, it can also be used without sponge. Because the pimples of long pips rubber are relatively slender, the phenomenon of reverse rotation can occur when hitting the ball, that is to say, in returning of a ball with heavy topspin or a powerful smash from an opponent, it makes the ball with backspin; when returning a no-spin ball, it is also a no-spin ball; in returning of a ball with backspin from an opponent, it makes the ball with topspin. The more spin a ball from an opponent is the stronger reverse rotation of returning becomes. Long pips rubber itself does not produce strong spin, but is mainly dependent on different spins of the coming ball to produce opposite spins. These abnormal changes will cause an opponent to make a fault or a high ball, creating a chance for you to attack.

图 1-9 长胶胶皮
Fig.1-9　Long pips rubber

（5）防弧圈胶皮。

防弧圈胶皮（如图 1-10）是一种专门对付弧圈球的胶皮。它看上去与反胶很相似，但这种胶皮面无黏性，表面较光滑且稍微发涩，击球速度较慢、弧线较短，着台后下沉飘忽，令对方难以按常规判断，对付弧圈球尤为奏效。

(5) Anti-spin rubber.

This is a kind of rubber sheet which is specially used to deal with loop. It looks very similar to the inverted rubber, but this kind of rubber is not sticky with a relatively smooth and slightly unsmooth surface. (As shown in fig.1-10) It hits the ball with a comparatively slower speed and a relatively short trajectory, and the ball will go down uncertainly after it touches the table, making it difficult for an opponent to form a judgment normally; it proves especially effective to deal with loop.

图 1-10 防弧圈胶皮
Fig.1-10　Anti-spin rubber

第二节
球拍的选择、粘贴与保养

球拍的型号和种类很多，它一般由底板、海绵和胶皮组成。专业选手或有一定水平的爱好者会根据自己的打法特点在专业体育器材商店选购适合自己的底板、海绵和胶皮（或套胶），然后自己粘贴。

1. 底板的选择

根据国际乒联的规则：底板应平整、坚硬，底板至少应含85%的天然木料。一块好的底板必须具备两个特点：一是击球时不感到底板震手，二是有较好的控制球的性能。每个人应根据自己的打法类型选择不同硬度的底板。一般近台快攻运动员可选用木质较硬的底板，以提高击球速度；以弧圈球为主要打法的运动员可选择木质较软、厚度稍薄的底板。而对于初学者，由于打法类型尚未确定，应选择重量较轻、手感较好、弹性略低的球拍，以便于尽快掌握控球技术。

Section 2
Choosing, gluing and maintenance of rackets

The table tennis racket which has many models and types, usually consists of a blade、a sponge and a rubber. According to the characteristics of their own playing styles, professional players or lovers with a certain level choose blades, sponges and rubbers (or sandwich rubbers) that are suitable for them in professional sports equipment shops, then glue rackets by themselves.

1. Choosing a blade

According to the ITTF regulations, a blade should be flat and rigid and it should contain at least 85% natural wood. A good blade must have two characteristics: first, when hitting the ball you do not feel the blade shaking your hand; second, it has good control performance of the ball. Everyone should choose different hardness of blade according to his playing style. Generally, athletes with close-table fast attack style can choose a blade of hard wood in order to improve the hitting speed; athletes who take loop drive as the main style can choose a slightly thinner blade of soft wood. For beginners, because their playing style has not yet been fixed, they should choose the blade of less weight and slightly lower elasticity which they feel good, so as to master the technique of controlling the ball as soon as possible.

2. 海绵与胶皮的选择

海绵和胶皮的种类有很多，选手应根据个人的打法特点配置适合自己的海绵与胶皮。选择海绵时，除了选择厚度和硬度之外，首先应观察其厚度是否一致，表面是否平整；然后把海绵放在硬的平面上用手指按压，好的海绵按下去应感觉柔和而且有弹性。选择胶皮时，首先要看颜色是否纯正，色彩是否均匀。其次，正胶要看颗粒上的花纹是否清晰，颗粒大小、行距间隙是否均匀；反胶要看胶皮皮面是否平坦，黏性是否合适。初学者尽量选用反胶或正胶等常规球拍，这样有利于全面学习技术。

2. Selection of sponge and rubber

There are many types of sponge and rubber. Players should choose sponges and rubbers which are suitable for themselves, based on the characteristics of individual playing style. Usually when choosing a sponge, first of all, you should observe whether its thickness is uniform and its surface is smooth, in addition to selecting thickness and hardness; then put the sponge on a hard flat surface to press it with fingers. A good sponge should be soft and elastic when it is pressed down. When choosing a rubber, you should firstly see whether its color is pure and uniform; second, for pips out rubbers, see whether the streaks on the pimples are clear, the sizes of the pimples and their spacing intervals are uniform; for inverted rubbers, see whether the surface is smooth and the stickiness is suitable for yourself. As far as possible, beginners should choose conventional rubber rackets such as inverted rubber rackets or pips out rubber rackets etc, which is conducive to learning the technique in an all-round way.

3. 球拍的粘贴

（1）反胶套胶拍的黏合程序（如图1-11）：

第一步：用胶水刷把胶水均匀地涂抹在海绵上；

第二步：在底板上均匀涂抹胶水；

第三步：将海绵和底板上的胶水晾干，用手背触摸海绵和底板感觉不粘手即可。双手拿住套胶的两侧，对准球拍，

3. Gluing a racket

(1) Gluing procedures for the inverted sponge(As shown in fig.1-11):

Step 1: daub glue evenly onto the sponge with a glue brush.

Step 2: daub glue evenly onto the blade.

Step 3: wait until the glue on the sponge and the blade to dry in the air; and that will do when touching the sponge and the blade with the back of hand, it is not sticky to the hand. Hold two sides of the inverted sponge

将套胶轻轻放置好，然后，用滚胶棒将套胶平整地粘贴在底板上，来回滚动几次，以保证粘贴牢固；

第四步：用剪刀沿着底板边缘剪下多余的胶皮，下剪时不要犹豫。剪好胶皮后，一个球拍就粘好了。

with both hands aiming it at the blade and put the sandwich rubber in place gently, then, use a pressure stick to glue it smooth onto the blade, rolling the pressure stick back and forth for several times, in order to assure gluing it firmly.

Step 4: use a scissors to cut out excess rubber along the edge of the blade; do not hesitate when cutting the rubber with a scissors. The work is done when the excess rubber is cut out.

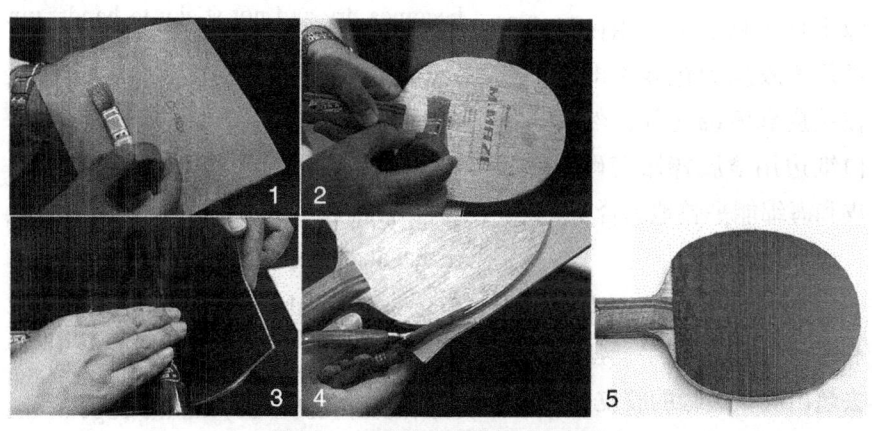

图1-11 反胶套胶拍的黏合程序

Fig.1-11 Gluing procedures for the inverted sponge

（2）用单海绵与反胶单胶片配置球拍的黏合程序：

第一步：分别在底板和海绵的一面均匀地涂上一层胶水；

第二步：待胶水晾干不粘手时将海绵与底板黏合，用滚胶棒（或类似的圆柱体，如擀面杖等）将海绵压实，剪去超出底板边缘的海绵；

(2) Procedures for gluing a racket with a separate sponge and a separate inverted rubber sheet:

Step 1: daub a layer of glue evenly onto one side of the blade and the sponge respectively.

Step 2: don't stick the sponge onto the blade until the glue is dry and not sticky to the hand. Compact the sponge with a pressure stick (or a similar cylinder, such as a rolling pin, etc.); cut out the excess sponge beyond the edge of the blade.

第三步：在海绵的另一面也均匀地涂上一层胶水，再把胶水均匀地涂在玻璃板上，然后将反贴胶皮轻轻平放上去，略用力均匀压实，稍等片刻使胶水均匀地粘到颗粒上；（注意：胶水不能流到颗粒的缝隙中，否则黏合后胶皮的表面会不平整。）

第四步：待海绵上的胶水晾干且不粘手后，用白纸或硬纸片（胶皮的包装物即可）垫在胶皮和海绵之间，然后边抽白纸边用滚胶棒跟着碾，使胶皮和海绵能平整地黏合；

第五步：用滚胶棒将胶皮和海绵压实、压平、压牢，剪去超出底板边缘的胶皮。（注意：一定要保留胶皮上的商标型号及国际乒联"ITTF"的标记。）

（3）用单海绵与正贴胶皮配置球拍的黏合程序：

海绵正贴胶皮拍的黏合过程与海绵反贴胶皮拍的黏合过程基本相同。只是第三步略有不同，因为是正贴胶皮拍，不需要通过玻璃板给胶皮上胶，直接在无颗粒胶皮面上均匀地

Step 3: daub a layer of glue evenly onto the other side of the sponge and a glass board; then gently put the inverted rubber sheet onto the coated glass board, with pips pointing downward, evenly compact it with slight force. Wait for a while and make the glue evenly stick onto the pimples. (Pay attention: do not let glue flow into the spacing intervals among the pimples, or else the surface of the rubber will not be flat after gluing it.)

Step 4: when the glue on the sponge becomes dry and not sticky to hands, put a blank sheet of paper or a cardboard (the packing materials for the rubber is ok) between the rubber sheet and the sponge. Then pull out the blank sheet of paper, at the same time follow it to press the rubber sheet with the pressure stick, making the rubber and the sponge glued evenly.

Step 5: press the rubber and the sponge with the pressure stick to make them firmly compacted and flatten; then cut out the excess rubber beyond the edge of the blade. (Pay attention: be sure to keep the trademark, the model and the mark of the international table tennis federation "the ITTF" on the rubber.)

(3) Procedures for gluing a racket with a separate sponge and a separate pips-out rubber sheet:

The procedures for gluing a racket with a separate sponge and a separate pips-out rubber sheet are basically the same as that of the procedures for gluing a racket with a separate sponge and a separate inverted rubber sheet. Only a slight difference is in the third step, there is no need to glue the rubber sheet by a glass board. Because it is a pips-

涂上一层胶水（不宜涂太厚）即可。

4. 球拍的保养

为了避免经常更换球拍给自己带来的不适应，同时减少不必要的开支，我们必须合理地使用球拍，并对球拍进行有效的保养，延长它的使用寿命。

（1）避免球拍在阳光下暴晒或离热源太近，否则容易使球拍的海绵和胶皮受热后老化，降低球拍的黏性和弹性。

（2）应保持球拍表面的清洁。打完球后，海绵反贴胶皮球拍可用洗胶液喷涂在胶皮表面，再用洗胶棉擦净；或用柔软的棉布蘸清水擦净，贴上护胶膜即可。千万不能把拍面放在水龙头下冲洗，以避免海绵的膨胀。而海绵正贴胶皮拍可用干净的布蘸清水把拍面上的脏污轻轻擦净、晾干。

（3）应防止非正常外力碰撞和挤压球拍。击球时，球拍要尽量避免磕碰球台。平时不用时最好将球拍放在专用的拍套里，以求最大限度地减少外力对球拍的挤压碰撞。

out rubber sheet, a even layer of glue (not too thick) can be directly coated on the side of the rubber sheet which has no pimples.

4．Maintenance of a racket

In order to avoid causing any inadaptation by frequently changing rackets, you must properly use the racket and give effective maintenance for it to prolong the service life of the racket. At the same time, unnecessary spending can be also reduced.

(1) You should avoid putting the racket in sun exposure or being too close to heat sources, which is easy to make the sponge and the rubber of the racket ageing and reduce the stickiness and elasticity of the racket.

(2) The surface of the racket should be kept clean. For a racket with inverted rubber, it spray the rubber cleaner on the surface after playing the ball, then wipe up with the special washing sponge for rubber or soft cotton cloth dipped in water; after that, attach a protective film to it. For goodness' sake, don't wash the surface of rackets under a tap to avoid the expansion of sponge. For a racket with pips-out rubber, gently wipe up dirt on the surface of the rubber with a clean cloth dipped in water then dry it in the air.

(3) Prevent non-normal external force from bumping and pressing the racket. When hitting the ball, avoid knocking against the table with the racket as far as possible. Usually, when the racket is not in use, it is best to put it in a special racket case in order to minimize the squeeze and bump from external force to the racket.

第二章
乒乓球基础知识
Chapter 2
Fundamental knowledge of table tennis

乒乓球基础知识内容分为基本姿势、基本站位、击球路线、击球时间、球拍触球部位、击球的部位及拍面角度等，掌握乒乓球的基础知识有助于学习认识乒乓球运动内在的规律，以便加强训练效果，提高比赛成绩。

第一节
基本姿势与站位

1. 基本姿势

两脚平行站立与肩同宽或略比肩宽，提踵，前脚掌内侧着地，两膝微屈、上体略向前倾；重心置于两脚之间，含胸收腹，两眼注视来球。执拍手臂自然弯曲，执拍于腹前，不执拍的手臂自然弯曲，置于腹前。（如图2-1）

The content of fundamental knowledge of table tennis is divided into the ready position, basic stance, paths of hitting the ball, time of hitting the ball, hitting spot on the racket、hit positions on the ball and racket angle, etc. Mastering the fundamental knowledge of table tennis is conducive to learning to know the inherent laws of table tennis, so as to strengthen the training effect and improve the competition results.

Section 1
Ready position and basic stance

1. Ready position

Two feet stand parallelly with shoulder width apart or slightly wider than shoulder-width; lift heels and make the inner side of forefeet touch the ground; both knees bend slightly and the upper body leans a little forward, putting the weight between the two feet. Keep the chest slightly inward and tuck in the stomach; two eyes gaze to the oncoming ball. The arm of racket hand should be bent naturally, and the racket should be placed in front of the stomach; the arm without the racket should also be bent naturally and put in front of the stomach. (As shown in fig.2-1)

图 2-1　基本姿势
Fig.2-1　Ready position

2. 基本站位

乒乓球的基本站位应根据不同类型的打法和个人特点确定。（如图 2-2）

2. Basic stance

The basic stance for table tennis should be determined according to different playing styles and individual characteristics. (As shown in fig.2-2)

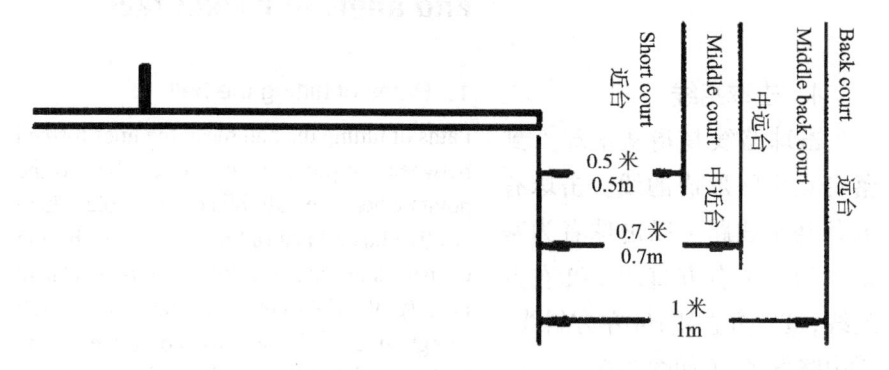

图 2-2　基本站位
Fig.2-2　Basic stance

一般有下列几种类型（以右手持拍为例）：

（1）左推右攻打法的运动员，其站位在近台中间偏左的位置。

（2）两面攻打法的运动员，其站位在近台中间的位置。

（3）弧圈球打法的运动员，其站位在中台中间偏左的位置。

（4）横拍攻削结合打法的运动员，其站位在中台附近。

（5）以削球为主打法的运动员，基本站位在中远台附近。

Generally speaking, there are several types of stance as listed below (taking the right-handed as an example):

(1) For athletes in the style of backhand block with forehand attack, the stance should be in the center-left of short court.

(2) For athletes in the style of two-winged attack, the stance should be in the center of short court.

(3) For athletes in the style of loop drive, the stance should be in the center-left of middle court.

(4) For athletes of shake-hand grip in the style of attack combined with chop, the stance should be near the middle court.

(5) For athletes in the style of chop, the stance should be near the middle back court.

第二节
击球路线、时间、部位与拍面角度

1. 击球路线

击球路线是指从击球点到落台点之间形成的线。击球有五条基本线路（以击球者为基准）为：①右方直线；②右方斜线；③左方直线；④左方斜线；⑤中路直线。（如图 2-3）

Section 2
Paths and time of hitting the ball, hitting spot on the ball and angle of racket face

1. Paths of hitting the ball

Paths of hitting the ball mean the lines formed between the points of hitting the ball to the points where the ball falls on the table. There are five basic lines (taking the player hitting the ball as the benchmark): ① the right straight line, ② the right crosscourt line, ③ the left straight line, ④ the left crosscourt line, ⑤ the middle straight line. (As shown in fig.2-3)

图 2-3 击球的五条基本线路
Fig.2-3 The five basic paths of hitting the ball

中路直线球在实际比赛中是随时以站位而定的，即追身球，也称中路追身路。

两条斜线有放射性的功能，读者朋友要充分运用和发挥它的这个作用。两条直线的作用在于两点：一是直线短，来球速度快，令对方防不胜防；二是训练时习惯练斜线。因此，对三条直线练得少的球员中线偏右的球实效性最好。

无论直拍还是横拍，中线球都是弱点，防守运动员最怕对方攻追身球，所以，平时五条线路都要训练，直线和中线要能运用自如，同时，也要学会回接对方打过来的球。

2. 击球时间

击球时间是指来球落台面弹起后，其运行轨迹从落台后上升再下降至触及地面以前的过程。大致可分为五个阶段（如图2-4）。

（1）上升期：来球从台面弹起至接近最高点的这段时间。上升期又可分

In the actual game, the middle straight line is decided by stance at any time, namely, body hit is also called as the middle straight line.

The two crosscourt lines have radiation function, which readers should sufficiently use and play its role. The role of the two straight lines lies in the two points: first, a straight line is short making the speed of an oncoming ball fast, which is impossible for an opponent to defend effectively; second, usually most players have a habit of practicing the crosscourt lines in training, therefore for players who practice less for the three straight lines, an oncoming ball to the position which is slightly off to the right of the center line has the best effectiveness.

For both pen-hold grip players and shake-hand grip players, it is the soft spot to return an oncoming ball from the middle straight line. Defensive players are most afraid of body hit attacking by opponents. Therefore, you should practice for all of the five lines in usual training, and can use the straight lines and the centre line with ease. At the same time, you should also learn to return the oncoming ball which is hit by an opponent from the straight lines.

2. Time of hitting the ball

Time of hitting the ball refers to the process which happens after a coming ball contacts your own playing surface and bounces up and before it hits the ground. The orbit of the ball includes ascending from the table to descending toward the ground. It can be roughly divided into five stages (As shown in fig.2-4).

(1) Ascending stage: it refers to the period of time during which the ball bounces from the table-board and ascends until it rises close to the peak. Ascending stage can be divided into early

为上升前期和上升后期。

上升前期：指来球从台面弹起后上升的最初一段。

上升后期：指球继续上升至高点期的一段。

（2）高点期：来球从台面弹起在最高点附近的这段时间。

（3）下降期：来球从最高点开始下降以后的这段时间。下降又可分为下降前期和下降后期。

下降前期：指球从高点期回落下降的最初一段。

下降后期：指继续下降至地面的一段。

ascending stage and late ascending stage.

Early ascending stage: it refers to the initial ascending period after the ball bounces up from the table-board.

Late ascending stage: it refers to the period during which the ball continues to ascend to the peak.

(2) Peak stage: it refers to the period of time during which the ball bounces up from the table-board and gets near the peak.

(3) Descending stage: it refers to the period of time during which the ball begins to descend from the peak. Descending stage can be divided into early descending stage and late descending stage.

Early descending stage: it refers to the initial descending period of the ball from the peak.

Late descending stage: it refers to the period during which the ball continues to descend to the ground.

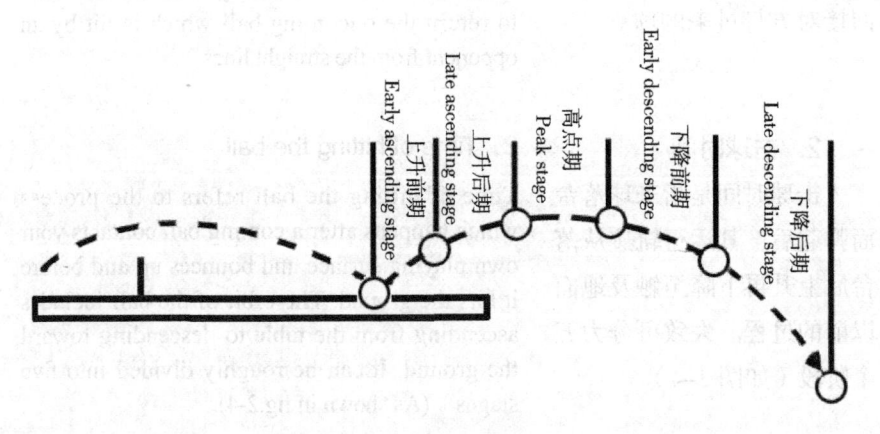

图 2-4 击球时间
Fig.2-4 Time of hitting the ball

3．球拍触球部位

球拍触球部位是指球拍触及球的部位。我们把球拍分成五个部分。上部：球拍触球的部位①；中上部：球拍触球的部位②；中部：球拍触球的部位③；中下部：球拍触球的部位④；下部：球拍触球的部位⑤。（如图 2-5）

3．Hitting spots on the racket

Hitting spots on the racket mean the parts on the racket which contact the ball. A racket can be divided into five parts. The upper part: it refers to ① on the racket which touches the ball. The middle-upper part: it refers to ② on the racket which contacts the ball. The middle part: it refers to ③ on the racket which contacts the ball. The middle-lower part: it refers to ④ on the racket which contacts the ball. The lower part: it refers to ⑤ on the racket which contacts the ball. (As shown in fig.2-5)

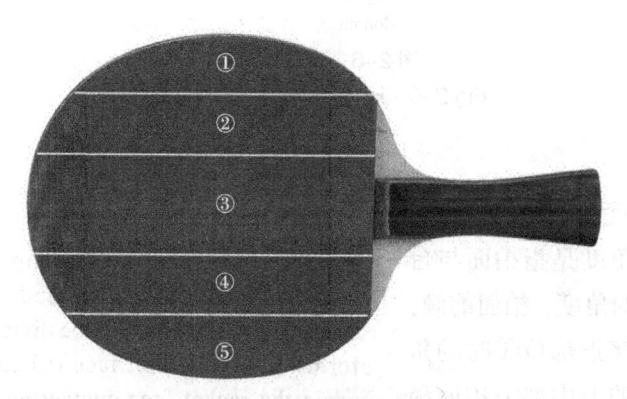

图 2-5　球拍触球部位
Fig.2-5　Hitting spots on the racket

4．击球的部位

在乒乓球技术中，我们通常把乒乓球分为七个部分，即：顶部、上中部、中上部、中部、中下部、下中部和底部。（如图 2-6）

4．Hit positions on the ball

In the table tennis techniques, a table tennis ball is usually divided into seven parts, which are hit positions on the ball, namely, the top, the top middle part, the middle-upper part, the middle part, the middle-lower part, the lower-middle part and the bottom. (As shown in fig.2-6)

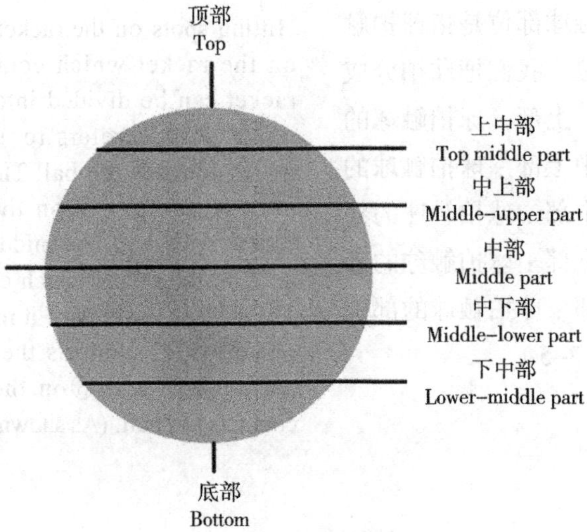

图2-6 击球的部位
Fig.2-6 Hit positions on the ball

5. 拍面角度

拍面角度是指拍面与台面所形成的角度，拍面前倾：拍面触球接近部位①时的角度，击球的上中部；拍面稍前倾：拍面触球接近部位②时的角度，击球的中上部；拍面垂直：拍面触球接近部位③时的角度，击球的中部；拍面稍后仰：拍面触球接近部位④时的角度，击球的中下部；拍面后仰：拍面触球接近部位⑤时的角度，击球的下中部。（如图2-7）

5. Racket angle

Racket angle refers to the angle which is formed by the racket face and the playing surface of the table. It can be divided into five forms. Closed racket face (tilted forward): when the racket face contacting the ball at the angle close to Position ①, it hits the top middle part on the ball. Slightly closed racket face: when the racket face contacting the ball at the angle close to Position ②, it hits the middle-upper part on the ball. Vertical racket face: when the racket face contacting the ball at the angle close to Position ③, it hits the middle part on the ball. Slightly opened racket face (slightly tilted backward): when the racket face contacting the ball at the angle close to Position ④, it hits the middle–lower part on the ball. Opened racket face: when the racket face contacting the ball at the angle close to Position ⑤, it hits the lower–middle part on the ball. (As shown in fig.2-7)

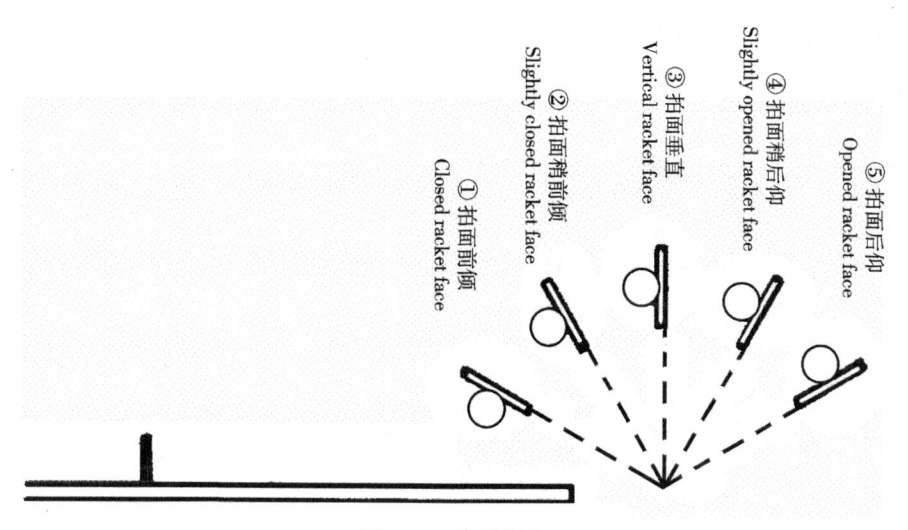

⑤ 拍面后仰 Opened racket face
④ 拍面稍后仰 Slightly opened racket face
③ 拍面垂直 Vertical racket face
② 拍面稍前倾 Slightly closed racket face
① 拍面前倾 Closed racket face

图 2-7 拍面角度
Fig.2-7 Racket angle

第三章
乒乓球的基本技术
Chapter 3
Basic techniques of table tennis

乒乓球的基本技术包括握拍方法、基本步法、过渡技术、发球与接发球技术、进攻技术、弧圈球技术和防守技术等。乒乓球基本技术对于乒乓球运动练习者是非常关键的，只有对基本技术进行规范化、系统化的训练才是走向专业化的唯一途径。

第一节
握拍法

乒乓球握拍方法分为横拍握法和直拍握法两种，不同的握法各有其特点，从而产生不同的打法。

1. 横拍握拍

横拍握拍法的特点是正反手攻球力量大，攻球和削球时握拍的手法变化小。反手攻球容易发力，也易于拉弧圈。但正反手交替击球时，需要变换击球拍面，动作偏大，影响摆臂速度，攻直线球时动作明显，易被对方识破。横拍握拍法如同握手一样。中指、无名指和小指自然握住拍柄，大拇指在球拍正面靠近中指，食指自然伸直，斜放于球拍背面。正手

The basic techniques of table tennis include ways of gripping the racket, basic footwork, transitional techniques, serve and receive, attack, loop drive and defensive techniques, etc. The basic techniques of table tennis are very critical for table tennis players. It is the only way to professionalization through standardized and systematic training for the basic techniques of table tennis.

Section 1
Ways to grip a racket

Ways of gripping a table tennis racket are divided into two types which are shake-hand grip and pen-hold grip. Each of the different grips has its own characteristics which result in different categories of playing style.

1. Shake-hand grip

Shake-hand grip features a powerful attack by both forehand and backhand. When attacking or chopping, the way of holding the racket has little change. It is easy to put forth the strength for backhand attack, and also apt to hit loop drive. But when attacking alternately with the forehand and backhand, you need to transform the hitting surface; the movement is too big, and affects the speed of swinging the arm. When attacking in a straight line, the obvious movement can be easily seen through by an opponent. Shake-hand grip is just like shaking hands. The middle finger, ring finger and little finger hold the handle of racket naturally; the thumb should be put on the front side and close to the middle finger, and the forefinger, which straightens naturally, should be put sideways

攻球时，食指稍向上移动；反手攻球时，拇指稍向上移动。（如图3-1）

on the back side of the racket. When attacking with the forehand, the forefinger should slightly move up; when attacking with the backhand, the thumb should slightly move up. (As shown in fig.3-1)

图 3-1　横拍握拍
Fig.3-1　Shake-hand grip

2. 直拍握拍法

直拍握拍法的特点是正反手都用球拍的同一面击球，出手快，正手击球快速有力，攻斜、直线球时，拍面变化不大，对手难以判断。但反手击球时，因受身体结构影响而不易发力，调节拍形亦较为困难，防守照顾面较小。握拍时，使拍柄贴在虎口上。球拍正面，食指、拇指自然弯曲，食指的第二指节和拇指的第一指节分别压住球拍两肩，食指与拇指间的距离要适中。球拍背面，中指、无名指、小指自然弯曲斜形重叠，以中指的第一指节侧面顶在球拍背面约1/3处。（如图3-2）

2. Pen-hold grip

Pen-hold grip has its own characteristics. Both forehand and backhand hit the ball with the same side of the racket, which provides fast speed of actions, fast and powerful forehand hit. When attacking with the forehand in a crosscourt line or in a straight line, the racket face has little change, which makes it difficult for an opponent to judge. But when hitting the ball with the backhand, it is not easy to put forth the strength due to obstruction of the body structure, and more difficult to adjust the angle of the racket; therefore it provides a smaller defensive area. When gripping the racket, put the handle on the thumb-index web; the forefinger and thumb bend naturally on the front side. The second joint of forefinger and the first joint of thumb press on the two shoulders of the racket respectively, with a moderate distance between the forefinger and thumb. The middle finger, ring finger and little finger naturally bend and overlap obliquely on the back side, and make the side of the first joint of the middle finger against the position which is about 1/3 of the racket back. (As shown in fig.3-2)

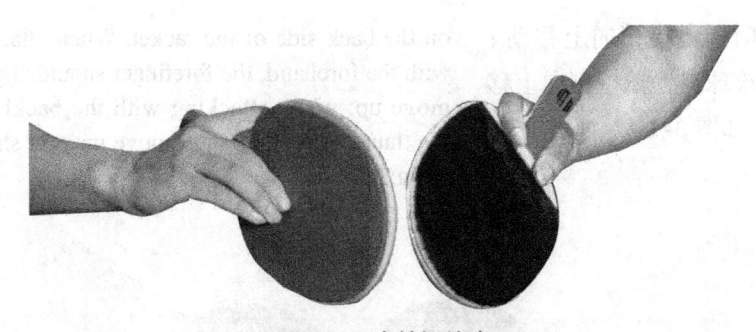

图 3-2 直拍握拍法
Fig.3-2 Pen-hold grip

3. 握拍时应注意的问题

（1）无论哪种握法，握拍都不应过紧或过松。过紧会影响击球的灵活性，过松则影响击球的力量和准确性。

（2）在变换击球的拍面、调节拍面角度时，要充分利用手指的作用。

（3）不应经常变换握拍方法，否则会影响打法类型及风格，尤其是初学者更应注意。

第二节
基本步法

乒乓球运动的发展使人们越来越重视步法的使用与训练，没有快速灵活的步法，就难以及时抢占有利的击球位置，并有效地回击来球。

3. Problems should be paid attention to when gripping the racket

(1) No matter what type of grip you use, holding the racket should not be too tight or too loose. Too tight grip will affect the flexibility of hitting the ball; too loose grip will affect power and accuracy of hitting the ball.

(2) When changing the racket face to hit the ball or adjusting its angle, you should make full use of the fingers' role.

(3) The way of gripping the racket should not be changed frequently, or else it will affect you playing type and style, which beginners should especially pay more attention to.

Section 2
Basic footwork

The development of table tennis makes players pay more and more attention to the use and training of footwork. It will be difficult to take up a favorable position of hitting the ball in time and effectively return an oncoming ball without quick and flexible footwork.

1. 单步

击球时以一只脚的前脚掌为轴，另一只脚根据来球方向移动一步，身体重心落在移动的脚上。（如图3-3）

1. Single step

When hitting the ball, take the forefoot of one foot as a pivot; and the other foot moves a step according to the direction of an oncoming ball, while the center of body weight falls on the moving foot. (As shown in fig.3-3)

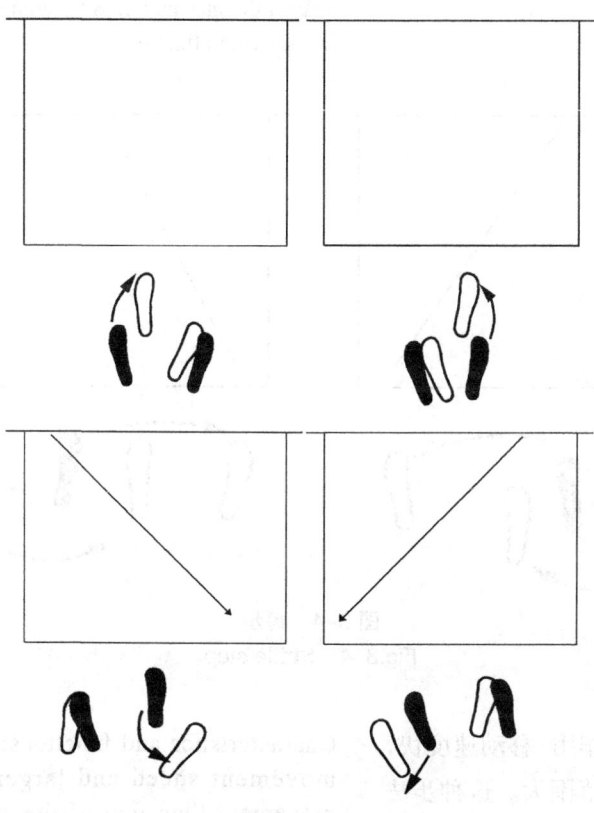

图 3-3 单步
Fig.3-3 Single step

特点与作用：动作简单灵活，重心转移较平稳。这种步法一般在来球角度不大的情况下采用，如近身的接发球、削追身球、单步侧身攻等。

Characteristics and functions: the movements are simple and flexible; the shift of weight is relatively stable. It is commonly adopted under such conditions in which the angle of an oncoming ball is not large; for instance, receiving a ball served close to the body, chopping a body hit, and a single-step sideways attack, etc.

2. 跨步

击球时以与来球不同方向的脚蹬地，另一只脚向来球方向跨出一大步，身体重心随即移至该脚，蹬地脚随后跟上一小步。（如图3-4）

2. Stride step

When hitting the ball, your foot which is in the different direction of the oncoming ball thrusts against the ground; the other foot moves a big step towards the direction of the oncoming ball shifting the weight immediately to the foot. Subsequently the foot which thrusts against the ground keeps up with a small step. (As shown in fig.3-4)

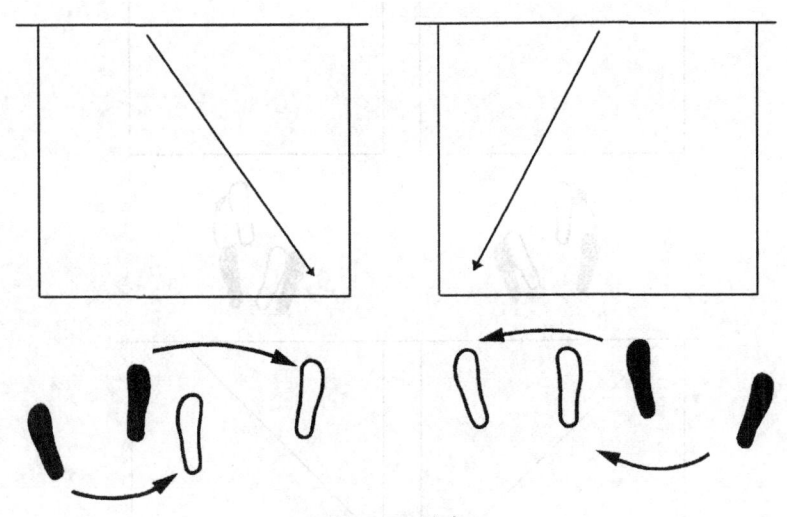

图 3-4 跨步
Fig.3-4 Stride step

特点与作用：移动速度快，比单步移动范围大。这种步法一般在来球速度快、离身体稍远时使用，适宜借力击球。例如，对方推挡连压反手后突然变正手，可运用跨步正手击球；削球打法时可左右移动击球。

Characteristics and functions: it has fast movement speed and larger range of movement than that of the single step. Generally, it is adopted for an oncoming ball with fast speed or a little farther away from the body. For example, an opponent suddenly changes the hitting line to your forehand after continuously striking to your backhand with block; you can adopt the stride step to hit the ball with forehand. Choppers can also adopt this kind of footwork to move right and left to hit the ball.

3. 并步

击球时一脚先向另一脚移一步，另一脚在移动的脚落地后再向来球方向移一步。（如图 3-5）

3. Side step

When hitting the ball, one foot first moves a step to the other foot, after the moving foot touches the ground, then the other foot moves a step in the direction of an oncoming ball. (As shown in fig.3-5)

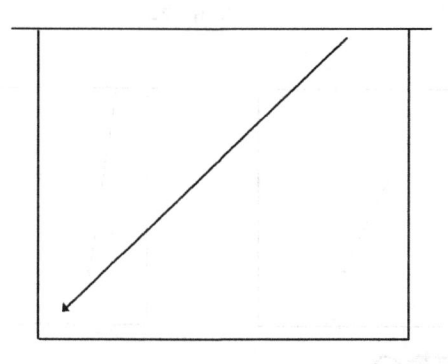

图 3-5 并步
Fig.3-5 Side step

特点与作用：移动时没有腾空动作，重心较平稳，移动范围较大。这种步法可连续使用，如左推右攻、左右削球、推挡侧身攻、小区域内连续走动进攻等。

Characteristics and functions: when moving, there is not any action of suspension, so the center of weight is relatively stable; and it can be used continuously due to larger range of movement. For example, the side step can be adopted for backhand block with forehand attack, chopping right and left, block with sideways attack and sequential moving attack in a small area and so on.

4. 跳步

击球时以来球不同方向的脚用力蹬地，两脚同时离地向来球方向跳动。（如图3-6）

4. Hop step

When hitting the ball, you should use the foot which is on the different side of an oncoming ball, to thrust hard against the ground, then two feet leave from the ground simultaneously and jump towards the direction of the oncoming ball. (As shown in fig.3-6)

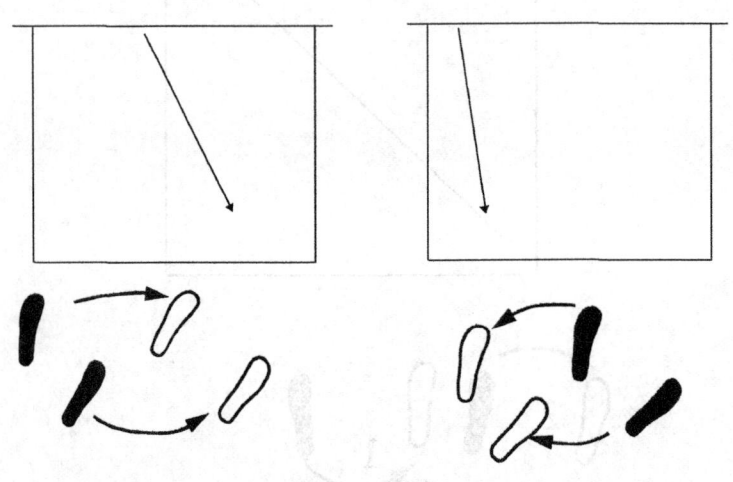

图 3-6 跳步
Fig.3-6 Hop step

特点与作用：移动范围比跨步大，有利于发力，移动后两脚间距离基本不变。这种步法适于连续运用，但移动时有短暂的腾空动作，对于保持身体重心的稳定有一定影响。跳步可用于连续发力击球，常与跨步结合起来使用，削球选手在接突击球和削追身球时常常使用。

Characteristics and functions: its movement range is larger than that of the stride step, and it is conducive to putting forth your strength. Because the distance between the two feet almost remains unchanged after movement, it is suitable for continuous use. But when moving, there is an action of short suspension, which will have a certain effect on maintaining the center of body weight stable. The hop step can be adopted for sequential powerful strokes, and is often used in combination with the stride step. When returning an oncoming ball of sudden and violent attack or chopping a body hit, choppers often adopt the hop step.

5. 交叉步

以来球同方向的脚为支撑脚，另一只脚在体前交叉，向来球方向跨一大步，然后支撑脚迅速跟上，移动一步。（如图3-7）

5. Crossover step

You should take the foot that is in the same direction of the oncoming ball as the supporting foot, and use the other foot to cross in front of the body making a big stride to the direction of the oncoming ball. And then the supporting foot moves a step quickly to keep pace with it. (As shown in fig.3-7)

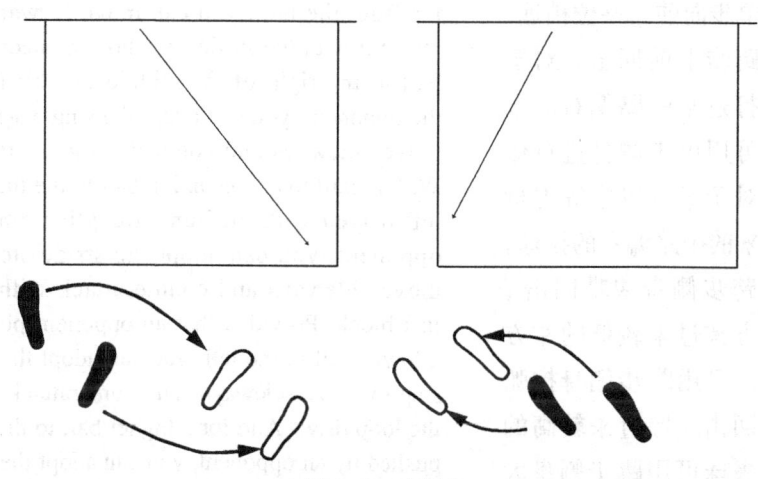

图 3-7 交叉步
Fig.3-7 Crossover step

特点与作用：交叉步移动范围最大，主要适合大角度击球使用。例如，快攻或弧圈打法在推挡或侧身攻后扑右角空当；或从右角变反手击球，在走动中前后或左右远距离削球等。

Characteristics and functions: the crossover step has the largest range of movement; and it is mainly suitable for hitting the ball with a large angle. For example, players of fast attack style or loop style rush at the empty position in the right-hand corner after block or sideways attack; or players change to backhand hitting from the right corner; and players move forward and backward or right and left to chop over a long distance and so on.

6. 步法的实际运用

在实践中，选手要根据对方来球的需要将上述各种基本步法的移动技巧结合运用，才能获得好的效果。一般在回击近网短球时，运动员站位较前，采用单步向前；站位稍远，采用跨步上前回击。对于对方打过来中路偏右的来球，可用单步侧身进行偷袭。对于对方以中等力量打过来的中路偏左的拉球，可用跨步侧身快带回击；若对方搓过来较低的左方来球，可用跳步侧身拉弧圈球回击。搓过来较高的左方来球可用跳步侧身大力扣杀。在相持时选手左右移动，快攻打法一般采用跨步结合跳步；弧圈打法一般多用连续跳步或跳步侧身接交叉步；削球打法则多用并步、跳步和交叉步结合使用。

在步法的结合使用时，要注意：一要保持身体的紧凑，不能松散，重心稳定；二要在步法与步法的衔接时，用小碎步进行调整；三要根据来球，以合适的

6. Practical application of footwork

In practice, players should combinatively use various movement skills of the basic footwork mentioned above according to the need of the oncoming ball from an opponent, which will obtain a good effect. Generally, when returning a drop shot, if your position is near the oncoming ball, you can move forward with the single step; if your position is a bit far from the ball, you can move forward to return it with the stride step. For an oncoming ball to the right of the middle line hit from the opponent, you can adopt the single step to move sideways and conduct a sneak attack. With regard to an oncoming ball to the middle left driven with medium strength from the opponent, you can adopt the stride step to move sideways and counterattack with the fast block. Provided that an opponent pushes a lower ball to the left, you can adopt the hop step to move sideways and counterattack with the loop drive. And for a higher ball to the left pushed by an opponent, you can adopt the hop step to move sideways and smash powerfully. At the stage locked in a stalemate, players of the fast attack style usually adopt the stride step in combination with the hop step to move left and right. Generally speaking, more players of the loop style use the hop step continuously or adopt the hop step sideways; then follow up with the crossover step. However, more choppers use the side step and the hop step in combination with the crossover step.

In the combined use of footwork, it should be noted that first, you should keep the body in a certain degree of tension and cannot be relaxed, and the center of weight should be stable; and second, when linking up one type of footwork with another type of footwork, you should adjust your position with small split steps; third, you should adopt appropriate

步法正确运用好腰、腿、脚的力量，转换好身体重心，做好脚、膝的蹬转动作。

第三节
过渡技术

过渡技术是在没有绝对有利进攻机会的情况下，采取的一个行之有效的方法。它不等同于消极防守，而是尽量形成主动进攻的手段。

1. 搓球技术

搓球是一项近台过渡性控球技术，一般用于回接下旋来球。比赛中通过它的节奏和旋转的变化可为进攻创造条件，甚至直接得分。它是初学削球时必须掌握的入门技术。搓球可分为正手搓球和反手搓球、慢搓和快搓、摆短、劈长、加转搓球和搓不转球。

（1）正手搓球。

身体站位近台偏右，左脚稍前，右脚稍后，两膝微屈。击球前，手臂外旋使拍面后仰，前臂向右后上方引拍；当来球跳至下降前期，前臂带动手腕

footwork according to the oncoming ball, and correctly use the power of your waist, legs and feet to shift the center of body weight well, completing the pushing and turning action of your feet and knees.

Section 3
Transitional techniques

Transitional techniques are the effectual ways that are used in the absence of absolute advantageous opportunities for offensive. They are not equal to the passive defense, but they are means to make as far as possible active attacks come into being.

1. Push technique

The push stroke is a kind of ball controlling technique in transition commonly used for returning the close-table oncoming ball of backspin. In the game, you can change the rhythm and spin of the push stroke to create the conditions for attacks and even score directly. It is the introductory technique which you must master when beginning to learn chopping. The push stroke can be divided into the forehand push and backhand push, the slow push and fast push, the drop-shot push and deep push, the heavy-spin push and no-spin push.

(1) Forehand push.

Your body position should be close to the table and deflect to the right; put the left foot a little bit in the front and the right foot slightly in the back; and both knees bend mildly. Before hitting the ball, your racket arm and hand turn outwards to tilt the racket face backward (open racket), the forearm

加速向前下方用力摩擦球,触球中下部。击球后,手臂继续随势向右前下方挥动并迅速还原。(如图3-8)

brings the racket towards the upper-right back direction. When the oncoming ball bounces to the early descending stage, your forearm should drive the wrist to accelerate grazing the ball forward and downward forcefully, contacting the middle-lower part of the ball. After hitting the ball, your racket hand and arm continue to move towards the lower-right front direction along with the inertia and quickly recover. (As shown in fig.3-8)

a. 横拍正手搓球
a. Forehand push with shake–hand grip

b. 直拍正手搓球
b. Forehand push with pen–hold grip

图 3-8　正手搓球
Fig.3-8　Forehand push

（2）反手搓球。

身体站位近台偏左，右脚稍前，左脚稍后，两膝微屈。当对方来球时，持拍手臂向左后上引拍，拍形稍后仰。击球时，前臂和手腕向前下方用力，同时配合内旋转腕动作，在来球的下降前期击球中下部。击球后，前臂随势前送并迅速还原。(如图3-9)

(2) Backhand push.

Your body position should be close to the table and deflect to the left, put the right foot a little bit in the front and the left foot slightly in the back; and both knees bend mildly. When the ball comes from the opponent, your racket hand and arm bring the racket towards the upper-left back direction, tilting the racket face backward (open racket). When hitting the ball, the forearm and wrist give strength forward and downward; at the same time the wrist turns inwards for coordination. When the oncoming ball bounces to the early descending stage, hit the middle-lower part of the ball. After hitting the ball, the forearm should move forwards along with the inertia and quickly recover. (As shown in fig.3-9)

a. 横拍反手搓球
a. Backhand push with shake–hand grip

b. 直拍反手搓球
b. Backhand push with pen–hold grip

图 3-9　反手搓球
Fig.3-9　Backhand push

（3）慢搓。

慢搓的动作幅度大，回球速度慢，有利于加强搓球的旋转。正手慢搓时，站位近台，距台约50厘米，右脚稍后，身体稍向右转。击球前，加大向右上方引拍的幅度；击球时，拍形稍后仰，手腕和前臂向左下方用力，在球下降期击球的中下部。反手慢搓时，击球前加大向左上方引拍的幅度，击球时拍形稍后仰，向右前下方用力，在球下降期击球的中下部。横拍选手应注意拇指和食指的协调发力。

（4）快搓。

对方过来的球不论是长球还是短球，你回过去的也不论是长球还是短球，只要是在球的上升期搓球，都叫快搓。

正手快搓时，身体站位近台偏右，右脚稍前。来球时，身体稍向右转，手臂稍向右前上引拍，肘部自然弯曲，手臂外旋使

(3) Slow push.

The movement range of the slow push is large and its speed of returning the ball is slow, which helps enhance spin of the push stroke. For the forehand slow push, your body position should be close to the table, namely about 50 centimeters away from it; besides, put the right foot a little bit in the back and the body slightly to the right. Before hitting the ball, increase the range of swinging the racket backward to the upper-right direction. When hitting the ball, tilt the racket a little bit backward; the wrist and forearm give strength towards the lower-left direction. When the oncoming ball bounces to the descending stage, hit the middle-lower part of the ball. For the backhand slow push, you should increase the range of swinging the racket backward to the upper-left direction before hitting the ball. When hitting the ball, you should tilt the racket a little bit backward, and give strength towards the lower-right front direction. When the oncoming ball bounces to the descending stage, hit the middle-lower part of the ball. Shake-hand grip players should pay attention to the coordination between the thumb and forefinger to put forth strength.

(4) Fast push.

No matter an oncoming ball from an opponent is long or short, and your returning ball is long or short, as long as you push the ball at the ascending stage, it is called the fast push.

For the forehand fast push, your body position should be close to the table and deflect to the right; put the right foot a little bit in the front. When the ball is oncoming, turn your body slightly to the right and the arm brings the racket slightly towards the upper-right front direction, the elbow bends naturally. Your racket hand and arm turn

拍面角度稍后仰，后引动作较小，当来球跳至上升期，利用上臂前送的力量，前臂与手腕配合，借力结合发力，触球中下部并向前下方用力摩擦。击球后，手臂随势前送并还原。

反手快搓时，站位左半台，左脚稍前，对方来球时，球拍稍向左后上方引拍，拍面稍后仰。当来球跳至上升期，以前臂发力为主，手腕配合，借力结合发力触球中下部向右前下方用力摩擦，击球后手臂随势前送并还原。快搓技术动作较小，速度较快，并且有一定的旋转，与其他搓球技术结合使用，能主动改变击球节奏，为力争主动创造条件。在完成这项技术时，除要正确运用快搓的方法外，还须注意加强对来球的判断，由于快搓击球时间早，击球时手臂要快速前伸迎球；注意与慢搓的区别，击球时手腕前送的幅度较小；站位不要离台太远，

outwards and tilt the racket face backward (open racket), taking back the racket with a smaller action. When the oncoming ball bounces to the ascending stage, you should take advantage of the onward strength by the upper arm; and make the forearm cooperate with the wrist to borrow strength and put forth strength in combination, contacting the middle-lower part of the ball and grazing the ball forward and downward forcefully. After hitting the ball, the arm and hand move forwards along with the inertia and quickly recover.

For the backhand fast push, your position should be in the left half court, and put the left foot a little bit in the front. When the ball is coming from the opponent, you should bring the racket slightly towards the upper-left back direction, tilting the racket face backward (open racket). When the oncoming ball bounces to the ascending stage, you should rely mainly on the forearm strength and cooperate with the wrist to borrow strength and put forth strength in combination, contacting the middle-lower part of the ball and forcefully grazing the ball toward the lower-right front direction. After hitting the ball, the arm and hand move forwards along with the inertia and quickly recover. With smaller movement of technique, faster speed and a certain spin, the fast push, which is used in combination with other push techniques, can proactively change the rhythm of hitting the ball to create conditions for gaining the initiative. When performing this technique, in addition to correctly using the way for fast push, you must also pay attention to intensifying the judgment for an oncoming ball. Because the time of hitting the ball for the fast push is early, when hitting the ball the arm and hand should stretch forward quickly to meet it. Pay attention to the difference

以免错过击球时机。

（5）摆短。

摆短是在快搓的基础上发展起来的一项技术，多用于接发球或对搓中。它具有速度快、弧线低、落点非常短的特点，控制对方抢攻抢位的作用显著。

摆短时，站位近台，重心前移，手臂前伸，使球拍接近来球的着台点，在上升前期击球。手腕和前臂结合用力，触球中下部，利用来球之力，将球轻"摆"至对方网前。其动作幅度很小。搓球注重旋转，而摆短不太注重旋转，只是调动对手。（如图3-10）

between the fast push and the slow push. When hitting the ball, the wrist should move forwards with a smaller range; your position should not be too far away from the table lest you misses the opportunity of hitting the ball.

(5) Drop-shot push.

The drop-shot push is a technique which is developed on the basis of the fast push; it is most used for serve receiving or counter push. With the characteristics of fast speed, low trajectory and very short placement, it has conspicuous effect of limiting an opponent to attack or loop first.

When performing the drop-shot push, your body position should be close to the table. Shift the center of weight forward, in the meantime, stretch the arm and hand forward to make the racket close to the landing point of the oncoming ball; and hit the ball at the early ascending stage. The wrist and forearm exert strength in combination to contact the middle-lower part of the ball, and lightly place the ball to the net zone of the opponent with a very small movement range, drawing support from the force of the oncoming ball. For pushing, you should lay emphasis on spin, but for the drop-shot push, you need not quite attach importance to spin, it is merely used to control the opponent. (As shown in fig.3-10)

1

2

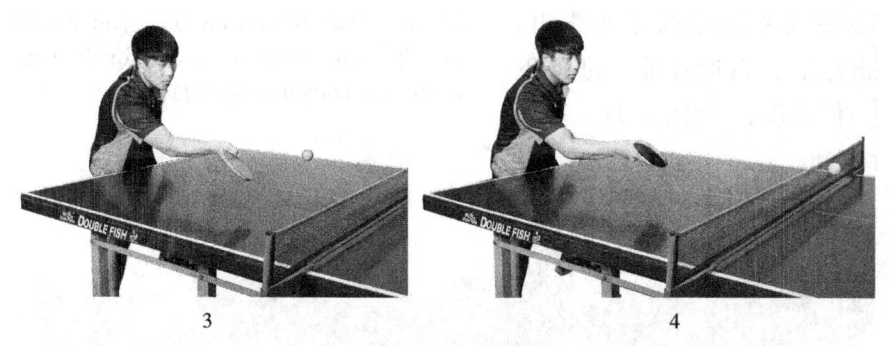

图 3-10 摆短
Fig.3-10 Drop-shot push

（6）劈长。

劈长速度快、线路长、旋转强，弧线低平，出手狠，落点往往直逼对方近端线处，常使对方无法获得上手进攻所必需的引拍距离，在接发球时与摆短配合运用能起到更好的效果。

劈长时，击球的上升期后段或前臂用力向前下方砍击，发力较集中。动作幅度比摆短大。

横板劈长，上身重心放低，前臂以及手腕向怀中内收，拍面后仰角比较小。击球时，前臂以及手腕迅速向前下方砍击，摩擦球的中下部。将爆发力全部作用在球上，加强发力。身体重

(6) Deep push.

With fast speed, long route, low and level trajectory, heavy spin and resolute shot, in most cases placement of the deep push is straight towards the location near the back line of an opponent usually making the opponent cannot get the backswing distance necessary for an attack. When receiving a serve, it is used cooperatively with the drop-shot push, which can have a better effect.

When performing the deep push, you should hit the ball at the late ascending stage, or put forth strength of the forearm to chop it forward and downward. The power should be relatively concentrated, and the movement range is larger than that of the drop-shot push.

For the backhand deep push with shake-hand grip, you should lower the centre of body weight and retract the forearm and wrist inside to your breast, with the angle of the racket face opened comparatively smaller. When hitting the ball, the forearm and wrist quickly chop it forward and downward, grazing the middle-lower part of the ball. You should strengthen the force and make the explosive force all act on the ball. The center of body weight should follow along toward the direction of grazing

心要随摩擦球的方向跟出。击球后，迅速还原，准备下一板进攻。（如图3-11）

the ball. After hitting the ball, you should quickly recover and get ready for the next attack. (As shown in fig.3-11)

图 3-11 劈长
Fig.3-11 Deep push

（7）搓转与不转球。

搓球时，用相似的手法可以搓出转和不转球，造成对方判断失误而争取主动或直接得分。搓转与不转球的动作方法与快搓、慢搓基本相同。主要区别是搓加转球时，增加球拍触球时间和面积，摩擦的成分为主；搓不转球时，球拍触球撞击或磕击的成分为主，向前将球托出。

(7) Heavy-spin push and no-spin push.

When performing a push, you can make the heavy-spin ball and no-spin ball with a similar technique, which will cause an opponent to make an error of judgment, to gain the initiative or score directly. The methods of movement for the heavy-spin push and no-spin push are basically the same as that of the fast push and slow push. The main difference is that you should increase the time and area of the contact between the racket and the ball, and attach most importance to friction when pushing the heavy-spin ball; but when pushing the no-spin ball, you should give priority to strike and knock for the contact of the racket to the ball, and carry the ball forward.

（8）搓球的练习方法。

①徒手模仿搓球动作。

②固定用慢搓或快搓接下旋球。

③对搓练习，先学反手，

(8) Training method of push.

①Use the racket hand to imitate the push action without the ball.

②Return a backspin service regularly with the fast push or the slow push.

③For the training of counter push, learn the

backhand push first, then learn the forehand push; and practice the slow push first, then practice the fast push.

④ Push the heavy-spin ball and the no-spin ball.

⑤ Push the ball with changed lines.

⑥ Practice pushing combined with attack after push.

⑦ In the practice of push, combine the fast and slow push with the deep push and the drop shot push.

2. Forehand fast block with shake-hand grip

(1) Characteristics and functions:

The technique of fast block, which can provide fast speed of actions, low trajectories and more changes in placement, and put forth strength in borrowing force, is more used with forehand. It is mainly used for coping with close-table returning loop drives, and lowering the quality of a return ball from an opponent, so as to change to take the initiative from a stalemate or a passive situation.

(2) Movement essentials:

Your body position should be close to the table, with your left foot slightly in the front and his upper arms close to the body. The arms and hands should be located above the horizontal plane of the table and bent naturally. When the ball is oncoming, tilt the racket face forward (closed racket face), and swing the racket back very little, almost in situ to approach the ball. The arm and wrist move towards front left to meet the ball, meanwhile the waist and hip begin to turn left. When the oncoming ball bounces

的转动，利用身体重心和手臂向前的力量，在借力中发力，击打中有稍向前摩擦的成分，手腕保持相对稳定不宜晃动。

（3）注意事项：

①站位不要远离球台，引拍动作不宜过大，否则会贻误最佳的击球时机，破坏整个动作的节奏，击球点偏后易导致失误。

②手腕如果乱晃，拍形就不易固定，如此将难以控制来球的旋转。

③不需突然的爆发力，而是用力比较平均，否则会影响击球的稳定性。

④主导思想上必须明确，快带只能作为过渡，目的是为了争取进攻的机会。因此，快带时须有清晰的战术意图，并且不宜过度使用，否则易导致被动。（如图 3-12）

to the ascending stage, tilt the racket face forward making the racket higher than the oncoming ball to hit the upper part of the ball; and utilize the center of body weight and the forward power of the arm to put forth strength in borrowing force with the help of the turning movement by the waist and hip. Hit the ball with slight friction forward, in the meantime keep the wrist relatively stable and do not shake.

(3) Matters needing attention:

① Your body position can not be far away from the table. The backswing action of the racket should not be too big, or else it will delay an optimal timing of hitting the ball, destructing the rhythm of the whole movement. A hitting point which is delayed will easily lead to misplay.

② If the wrist sways disorderly, the angle of the racket cannot be easily fixed; and in this way it will be hard to control the spin of an oncoming ball.

③ You needn't suddenly provide an explosive force, but give an average force; otherwise it will affect the stability of hitting the ball.

④ The dominant idea must be clear, namely take the fast block only as a transition whose purpose is to seek for an opportunity to attack. Therefore, when using the technique of fast block, you must have a clear tactical intention and should not overuse it, or it is prone to result in passiveness. (As shown in fig.3-12)

图 3-12　横拍正手快带
Fig.3-12　Forehand fast block with shake-hand grip

3. 横拍反手快带技术

击球时，在来球的上升期，向斜前方击球的中上部，击球瞬间手腕相对稳定。击球后前臂继续摆动，迅速还原。（如图 3-13）

3. Backhand fast block with shake-hand grip

When hitting the ball, you should hit the middle-upper part of it towards the oblique front at the ascending stage of the oncoming ball. The wrist should be relatively stable at the moment of hitting the ball; and after hitting the ball the forearm should continue to swing and quickly recover. (As shown in fig.3-13)

图 3-13　横拍反手快带
Fig.3-13　Backhand fast block with shake-hand grip

4. 横拍反手快拨技术

特点与作用：具有站位近台，动作小，球速快的特点，是用来对付上旋来球的一项相持性技术。在比赛中，能扩大主动进攻范围，是横拍握法选手最常用一种基本技术。

击球前，双脚平行站立，上体稍前倾，收腹含胸，两腿弯曲，脚跟微微上提。重心下沉，持拍手略高于台面，大臂与上体的夹角约30~40度，右肩微下沉。球拍保持在台面上，置于胸前下方。将球拍引至体前偏左侧，拍头朝左。击球时，重心移至右脚，以肘为轴，拍面前倾，在球的上升期击球的中上部，借助来球的反弹力，前臂手腕迅速前伸外展，向右前上方发力。击球后，前臂继续摆动，随后快速还原。（如图3-14）

4. Backhand fast flick with shake-hand grip

Characteristics and functions: The backhand fast flick with close-table positions, small movements and fast ball speed, is a technique of the sustained rally which is used for coping with an oncoming ball of top spin. In the game it can expand the scope of active attacks, and is a basic technique most commonly used by players with shake-hand grip.

Before hitting the ball, both feet stand parallelly, and the upper body slightly leans forward; draw the abdomen in and keep the chest a little inward; both legs bend and the heels lift a bit. Lower down the center of weight, and the racket hand is slightly higher than the table-board with an angle about 30~40 degrees between the upper arm and the upper body; and the right shoulder sinks a bit. Keep the racket above the table and below the chest. Swing the racket to the front-left of the body with the racket head towards the left. When hitting the ball, transfer the center of weight onto the right foot, and take the elbow as a pivot with the racket face tilted forward (closed racket face); and hit the middle-upper part of the ball at its ascending stage; with the help of the counterforce from the oncoming ball, the forearm and wrist protract and extend promptly to put forth strength towards the upper-right front direction. After hitting the ball, the forearm should continue to swing and then quickly recover. (As shown in fig.3-14)

1　　　　　　　　2　　　　　　　　3

a. 横拍反手快拨
a.Backhand fast flick with shake-hand grip

1　　　　　　　　2　　　　　　　　3

b. 直拍反手快拨
b.Backhand fast flick with pen-hold grip

图 3-14 反手快拨
Fig.3-14　Backhand fast flick

快带和快拨不是一回事，它们的主要区别是：快带手腕发力成分小；快拨手腕发力成分大，因而威力更强。但是当遇到弧圈球等强烈的上旋球时，使用快拨难度较大，成功率不高，而运用快带技术则较有把握。但在对付推挡、攻球或其他旋转不强

The fast block and the fast flick are not the same thing, and the main difference between them reads as follows. When performing the fast block, the wrist should put forth lesser strength; but for the fast flick, the wrist should put forth greater strength; therefore it is more powerful. However, when encountering an oncoming ball with strong topspin such as loop, etc., it is relatively more difficult to use the technique of fast flick whose success rate in such cases is not high; yet use the technique of fast block with more certain of success. But in coping with the block and the attack or other topspin balls whose

的上旋球时，运用快拨技术速度更快，力量也更大一些，因而相对来说较为有利。

5. 直拍推挡技术

直拍推挡球是进攻打法中的一项控制性技术。它既能成为争取主动的助攻手段，又能起到积极防御或从相持变为主动的作用。直拍推挡分为挡球、快推、加力推、减力挡、推挤、下旋推挡以及正手推挡。

（1）推挡球的基本技术。

推挡者一般站在离台30~50厘米的左半台的1/3处，两脚平行站立或左脚稍前，上臂和肘部自然弯曲并靠近身体右侧，拍面与台面近乎垂直，肩部放松。反手推挡时，要拇指放松，食指压拍，中指第一个关节顶拍，虎口和拍柄有一点空隙，引拍的时候在腹前，由后向前上推，手腕相对固定，不要用太多手腕，略加一点点手腕。（如图3-15）

spin is not strong, relatively speaking, it is advantageous to use the technique of fast flick which has faster speed and stronger force.

5. Block with pen-hold grip

The block with pen-hold grip is a technique of control in the attacking style. It can be a supporting tool to gain the initiative and play a role in an aggressive defense or turning the situation from a sustained rally into the initiative as well. The block with pen-hold grip is divided into the block, the fast block, the accentuated block, the stop block, the shoving block, the chop block and the forehand block.

(1) The basic technique of block.

Generally, a blocker should stand at 1/3 of the left half court and about 30 ~ 50 cm away from the table. Two feet stand in parallel or put the left foot slightly in the front; at the same time the upper arm and elbow bend naturally and close to the right side of the body with the racket face approximately vertical to the table-board and the shoulders relaxed. For the backhand block, relax the thumb and use the forefinger to press the racket with the first joint of the middle finger against the racket and a little gap between the thumb-index web and the handle of racket. Swing back the racket in front of the abdomen, and then push forwards and upwards from the back with the wrist relatively fixed. Don't use the wrist too much, and use it slightly. (As shown in fig.3-15)

图 3-15　直拍反手推挡
Fig.3-15　Backhand block with pen-hold grip

（2）挡球。

回球速度慢、力量轻，动作简单，初学者容易掌握。击球时，前臂稍向前移动，在来球的上升期击球的中部，借助来球的力量将球挡回。

（3）快推。

回球速度快、线路变化多，能袭击对方空当。击球前，持拍手肘关节靠近身体，前臂略外旋；击球时，前臂主动、迅速前迎，触球瞬间手腕外旋，拍形稍前倾，在上升期触球的中上部。

（4）加力推。

回球速度快、力量重,击球点较高。击球前，

(2) Block.

With a slow speed of returning the ball, light force and simple movements, the block is easy for beginners to master. When hitting the ball, the forearm should slightly move forward to hit the middle part of the ball at its ascending stage; and rely on the power of the oncoming ball to block the ball back.

(3) Fast block.

The fast block which provides a fast speed of returning the ball and more changes in returning lines can be used to attack the empty position of an opponent. Before hitting the ball, the elbow joint of the racket hand should be close to the body with the forearm slightly turning outward. When hitting the ball, the forearm should move forwards actively and quickly to meet the oncoming ball; and in the instant of contacting the ball the wrist should turn outward tilting angle of the racket forwards (closed racket face), to contact the middle-upper part of the ball at its ascending stage.

(4) Accentuated block.

The accentuated block with a higher hitting point provides a fast speed of returning the ball and heavy force. Before hitting the ball, raise the center

身体重心提高，前臂上提，球拍后引，略高于来球，拍面前倾。击球时，前臂用力向前下方推压，在球的上升后期或高点期击球的中上部。触球时，拍后三指用力顶拍，重心前移；击球后手臂随势伸直。

of body weight and lift the forearm; swing the racket backwards and make it a little higher than the oncoming ball with the racket face tilted forward (closed racket face). When hitting the ball, put forth the forearm's strength to push and press forward and downward, hitting the middle-upper part of the ball at its late ascending stage or the peak stage. When contacting the ball, put the three fingers behind the racket against it forcibly and shift the center of body weight forward. After hitting the ball, straighten the arm along with the inertia.

（5）减力挡。

减力挡回球弧线低、力量轻、落点近，常用于对付加转弧圈球和两面攻选手。击球前持拍手臂向前迎球，在球拍触球瞬间，球拍适度后缩，减弱来球的反弹力。实践中，多与加力推结合使用，可以前后调动对方，相得益彰。

(5) Stop-block shot.

Returning the oncoming ball with the stop-block shot, it will provide a low trajectory, light force and short placement. The stop-block shot is commonly used to cope with the players of heavy-spin loop and two-winged attack. Before hitting the ball, the racket hand and arm should move forward to meet the ball; and in the instant of contacting the ball, retract the racket moderately to weaken the bounciness of an oncoming ball. In practice, it is most used in combination with the accentuated block, complementing each other, which can force an opponent to move forward and backward.

（6）推挤。

推挤主要用于对付弧圈球。推出去的球带有侧下旋，角度大，弧线低，还有点发飘。虽能为进攻制造转机，但因其速度较慢，最好能与加力推或反手攻结合运用。

当球在上升期，触球的左侧中上部，沿球体向左下方用力，以摩擦为主

(6) Shoving block.

The shoving block is mainly used for coping with the loop. Its return can produce side backspin, large angle and low trajectory and is erratic in a way. Although it can make a turnaround for attack, its speed is relatively slow. So it is better to use the shoving block in combination with the accentuated block and backhand attack.

When the oncoming ball bounces to the ascending stage contact the middle-upper part on the left side of the ball and put forth strength along the sphere towards the lower left, giving

（挤擦球体）。触球瞬间，中指应用力顶住球拍。

推挤加转弧圈球时，球拍应在身体重心的带动下向前迎球，球拍稍高于来球，拇指放松，食指压迫，拍形前倾（大约与台面成50°角）。（如图3-16）

priority to friction (shove and rub the sphere). In the instant of contacting the ball, the middle finger should be put against the racket forcibly.

When returning an oncoming ball of heavy-spin loop with the shoving block, you should move the racket forward driven by the center of body weight to meet the oncoming ball, making the racket a little higher than the oncoming ball. At the same time relax the thumb and use the forefinger to press the racket, tilting the racket face forward (about the 50° angle to the table-board). (As shown in fig.3-16)

图 3-16 推挤
Fig.3-16 Shoving block

（7）下旋推挡。

下旋推挡：推过去的球速度快且急，并带下旋，对方若不适应易陷入被动或失误。主要用于助攻或积极相持阶段，通过变化回球旋转来争取主动。

运用时球拍略高于来球，拍形稍后仰。在来球的高点期或上升期后段触球的中下部，以前臂发力

(7) Chop block.

The chop block can produce some backspin and its return is fast and fierce. If an opponent does not adapt to it, he will be prone to fall into the passiveness or lead to errors. Therefore, it is mainly used for assisting attacks or gaining the initiative through changed spin of its return in an active stalemate stage.

When applying the chop block, make the racket a little higher than the oncoming ball with the racket face slightly tilted backward. Contact the middle-lower part of the ball at its peak stage or the late ascending stage; and forcefully push and

为主，向前下方用力推切，使回球弧线低且下沉。手腕在触球瞬间，可适当配合前臂向前下方用力切球，以增大回球的下旋力和速度，但手腕不要转动。

（8）正手推挡。

当对方拉弧圈球至我方正手，或遇到对方攻我方正手位的速度很快的来球时，用正手推挡过渡一板，比较保险。该技术的特点是，动作简单易掌握，回球稳健。对此技术的要求是，回球弧线要低，应控制好落点。

站位近台。击球前，前臂稍抬起，身体重心略升高，球拍略高于或同高于来球。触球时，自己发力较小，以借来球力为主，手腕和前臂应保持适宜的紧张度，拍形固定，基本与台面垂直或稍前倾。

在来球上升期击球，触球的中部或中上部。注意运用身体重心来控制击球弧线。（如图3-17）

chop it forward and downward giving priority to the forearm strength, which will make the return with low trajectory and a down force. In the instant of contacting the ball, the wrist can cooperate with the forearm properly to chop it forward and downward forcefully, so as to increase the backspin force and speed of the return. Nevertheless don't turn the wrist.

(8) Forehand block.

When an opponent does a loop drive to your forehand position or attacks your forehand position with very fast speed, it is comparatively secured to play a stroke with the forehand block as a transition. The characteristics of the technique are that its actions are simple, which is easy to grasp, and its return is steady. This technique requires that the trajectory of its return should be low and its placement should be controlled well.

The body position should be close to the table. Before hitting the ball, raise the forearm a little and lift the centre of body weight slightly, making the racket slightly higher than the oncoming ball or with the same height to it. When contacting the ball, you should put forth lesser strength, giving priority to borrowing force from the oncoming ball. In the meantime the wrist and forearm should keep appropriate tensity; and make the angle of racket fixed, basically vertical with the table-board or tilted a little forward (closed racket).

You should hit an oncoming ball at its ascending stage, contacting the middle or the middle-upper part of the ball; and pay attention, use the center of body weight to control the trajectory of hitting the ball. (As shown in fig.3-17)

图 3-17 正手推挡
Fig.3-17 Forehand block

（9）推挡球的练习方法。

①徒手模仿练习和两人台上对练挡球，体会动作要领。

②左方斜线对推练习，逐渐加速和加力，主要是让练习者体会手腕前臂的动作。

③推斜线，再对推直线，速度逐渐加快。

④推挡对左推右攻。

⑤推 2/3 台或全台对正手攻。

⑥推挡变线。

(9) Training methods for block.

① Use the racket hand to imitate the block action without the ball, and two people practice counter-block on the table experiencing the essentials of movement.

② Practice counter-block in the left crosscourt line, gradually speed up and increase the force, which mainly makes the learners experience the movements of the arm and wrist.

③ Block in the crosscourt line first, then block to counter block in the straight line, accelerating gradually.

④ Use the block to counter the backhand block with forehand attack.

⑤ Use the block to counter the forehand attack in 2/3 court or in the full court.

⑥ Block to change hitting lines.

第四节
发球技术

发球是乒乓球比赛中每一个回合的开始，它是乒乓球技术中唯一不受对方干扰和限制的技术，可以最大限度地满足自己的愿望和战术意图，先发制人，为整个战局创造有利条件。

1. 平击发球

特点：平击发球基本不带旋转，球平动式前进，可使初学者了解发球规则，是学习其他发球技术的基础。

发球要点：正手发平击球时，站位近台，右脚稍后，重心在右脚，执球手与执拍手均在身体右侧前方；抛球后，执拍手稍向后引拍，拍形稍前倾，球下降至约与球网同高时，触球中部，向前挥拍，重心前移至左脚。反手发平击球时，站位近台、中线偏左，左脚略后，抛球后右手向身体左后方引拍，拍形垂直，球与网同高时，

Section 4
Serve techniques

Serve is the beginning of each round in a table tennis match. It is the only technique in table tennis which is not affected by the interference and restriction of an opponent, and it can satisfy your own desire and tactical intention in a maximum limit, forestalling the opponent to create favorable conditions for the whole game.

1. Flat serve

Characteristics as follows: the flat serve is basically of no spin and makes the ball go forward in the translational type, which can make beginners understand the rules for serve and is the basis of learning other techniques of serves.

The serve essentials: when playing the flat serve with the forehand, your body position should be close to the table, with the right foot slightly in the back and the center of your body weight on the right foot. Put both the hand holding the ball and the racket hand in the right front of the body. After tossing the ball, you should swing the racket hand backward slightly, tilting the racket face a bit forward. When the ball falls to around the same height with the net, you should swing the racket forward and contact the middle part of the ball, shifting the center of your body weight forward to the left foot. When playing the flat serve with the backhand, your body position should be close to the table and slightly off to the left of the center line with the left foot slightly in

右臂向右前方发力，击球中部。(如图 3-18)

the back. After tossing the ball, swing the racket backward to the left back of the body with the right hand making the angle of the racket in vertical position. When the ball falls to around the same height with the net, put forth the strength of the right arm toward the right front of the body to hit the middle part of the ball. (As shown in fig.3-18)

a. 正手平击发球
a. Forehand flat serve

b. 反手平击发球
b. Backhand flat serve

图 3-18　平击发球
Fig.3-18　Flat serve

2. 正手发奔球

特点：球速快、线路长、冲力大，发至对方大角或中路偏左的位置，给对方较大威胁。

2. Forehand deep topspin serve

Characteristics as follows: the forehand deep topspin serve which is provided with fast ball speed, a long line and a strong impulse force, will give a larger threat to an opponent if it is served to the corners or the left-of-centerline of the opponent's table.

发球要点：左脚稍前，身体稍向右转，球向上抛起后，执拍手随即向后上方引拍，击球时前臂快速由后向左前方挥动，拇指压拍，拍面稍前倾并略向左方偏斜，球拍沿球的右侧中部向中上部摩擦；击球后，前臂和手腕随势向前挥动。（如图 3-19）

The serve essentials: put the left foot slightly in the front with the body a little bit to the right. After tossing up the ball you should swing the racket hand backwards and upwards immediately. When hitting the ball, swing the forearm quickly from the back toward the left front, and use the thumb to press the racket with the racket face slightly tilted forward and leaned a bit to the left; meanwhile make the racket graze the ball along the middle part of its right side toward the middle-upper part. After hitting the ball, the forearm and wrist swing forward along with the inertia. (As shown in fig.3-19)

图 3-19　正手发奔球
Fig.3-19　Forehand deep topspin serve

3. 反手发急球

特点：球速急、弧线低、前冲大，迫使对方退台接球，有利于抢攻。

3. Backhand fast serve

Characteristics as follows: the backhand fast serve, which is provided with fast ball speed, low trajectory and a large forward momentum, can force an opponent to back to receive the ball, which helps you launch an attack first.

发球要点：左脚稍后，身体稍向左转，击球时，执拍手以肘关节为中心，前臂向右前方横摆发力击球，拍面稍前倾，击球的中上部；击球后，前臂

The serve essentials: put the left foot slightly in the back with the body turning a little bit to the left. When hitting the ball, you should take the elbow joint of the racket hand as a pivot; and swing the forearm transversely toward the right front. Hit the middle-upper part of the

和手腕随势向前挥动。发急下旋球时，大拇指用力压球拍的左肩，使拍面稍后仰；触球前，稍向左后上方引拍；当球下降至低于网时，前臂快速向前下方用力，拍面触球的中下部；触球瞬间，手腕附加爆发式下切动作。（如图 3-20）

ball forcefully with the racket face tilted slightly forward. After hitting the ball, the forearm and wrist swing forward along with the inertia. When making the fast backspin serve, use the thumb forcefully to press on the left shoulder of the racket, making the racket face tilted backward slightly. Before contacting the ball, swing the racket back a bit toward the upper-left back direction. When the ball falls below the net, the forearm exerts strength quickly forwards and downwards, with the racket face contacting the middle-lower part of the ball. In the instant of contacting the ball, the wrist should add an action of chopping explosively.(As shown in fig.3-20)

图 3-20　反手发急球

Fig.3-20　Backhand fast serve

4. 发短球

特点：击球动作小，出手快，球落到对方台面后的第二跳不出台，使对方不易发力抢拉、冲或抢攻。

4. Short serve

Characteristics as follows: the short serve is provided with the small action of hitting, fast movement speed, and short placement. After the ball falls onto the table-board of an opponent and bounces twice it will not go outside the table, which makes it difficult for the opponent to loop or attack first.

发球要点：主要靠手腕和前臂摩擦发力，控制向前的力量。击球时，手腕的力量大于前臂的力量，发球的第一落点不要离网太近。

5. 发下旋球

（1）正手发下旋球，站位近台偏左角，左脚在前，右脚在后，左手持球置于掌心向上抛起，同时右臂外旋，向右后上方引拍。当球从高点下降至稍高于网或与网同高时，前臂加速向左前下方发力，同时手腕屈并内收，以球拍远端（拍头）触球，击球中下部向底部摩擦。击球后，手臂继续向左前下方随势挥动。（如图3-21）

The serve essentials: you should mainly use the wrist and forearm to put forth frictional force, and control the power of forward. When hitting the ball, the strength of the wrist should be greater than that of the forearm; and do not make the first placement of the ball too close to the net.

5. Backspin serve

(1) Forehand backspin serve: your body position should be close to the table and deflect to the left corner; and put the left foot in the front and the right foot in the back. Use the left hand to hold the ball in the palm and throw it up; at the same time turn the right arm outward swinging the racket back toward the upper-right back direction. When the ball falls to the height that is a little higher than the net or to the same height with the net, the forearm should speed up to put strength toward the lower-left front direction. Meanwhile you should bend the wrist and turn it inward, and contact the ball with the distal end (racket head), hitting the middle lower part of the ball and grazing toward its bottom. After hitting the ball, the forearm and wrist should continue to swing toward the lower-left front direction along with the inertia. (As shown in fig.3-21)

1   2   3   4

图3-21　正手发下旋球

Fig.3-21　Forehand backspin serve

（2）反手发下旋球，站位近台偏左角，右脚在前，左脚略后。左手持球置于掌心向上抛起，同时右臂内旋。直握拍手腕做弯曲运动，使手向掌心方向弯曲；横握拍手腕略向外展，使拍面稍后仰，向左后方引拍，当球从高点下降至稍高于球网或与网同高时，前臂加速向右前下方发力，同时直握拍手腕做伸展动作，横握拍手腕内收，以球拍远端（拍头）触球，击球中下部向底部摩擦。击球后手臂继续向右前下方随势挥动。（如图3-22）

(2) Backhand backspin serve: your body position should be close to the table and deflect to the left corner; and put the right foot in the front and the left foot slightly in the back. Use the left hand to hold the ball in the palm and throw it up, in the meantime turn the right arm inwards. For players of pen-hold grip, the wrist should do a bending motion making the hand crook toward the center of the palm. For players of shake-hand grip, the wrist should slightly abduct to make the racket face tilted backward a little (opened racket face); and swing the racket toward the left back direction. When the ball falls from the peak to the height that is a little higher than the net or to the same height with the net, the forearm should speed up to put strength toward the lower-right front direction. Meanwhile for the pen-hold grip, the wrist should do a stretching motion; and for the shake-hand grip, the wrist should retract inwards to contact the ball with the distal end (racket head), hitting the middle-lower part of the ball and grazing toward its bottom. After hitting the ball, the forearm and wrist should continue to swing toward the lower-right front direction along with the inertia. (As shown in fig.3-22)

图 3-22　反手发下旋球
Fig.3-22　Backhand backspin serve

下旋发球在比赛中使用率很高，许多选手运用强烈的下旋发球配合相似手法的不转发球迷惑对手，造成对方判断错误，为进攻创造机会。采用正、反手发下旋球时，质量的高低取决于发球时发力部位，以前臂、手腕和手指为主，尤其中指的发力和触球瞬间爆发的摩擦力一定要集中，拍面较后仰，摩擦的角度要适宜。正手动作要注意前臂由屈到伸用力。反手发球由于受身体限制，应充分发挥收腹、转腰的协调用力作用。

The utilization rate of the backspin serves is very high in the game. Many players use the heavy backspin serves together with the no-spin serves in similar techniques to confuse the opponents, and easily cause misjudgments of the opponents creating opportunities to attack. For the forehand backspin serve and the backhand backspin serve, whether the quality of the serves is high or low depends on the parts which put forth strength when serving a ball. For which the priority should be given to the forearm, wrist and fingers; and especially the strength put forth by the middle finger and the explosive force of friction must be concentrated in the instant of contacting the ball. Simultaneously, the racket face should be relatively tilted backward (opened racket face) making an appropriate angle of friction. You should pay attention to the forehand movement which put forth strength by the forearm from bending to stretching. And for the backhand serve, due to the physical limit of the body, you should give full play to the coordinating role of drawing in the abdomen and turning the waist.

6. 发不转球

（1）正手发不转球时，站位与正手发下旋球一样，左手将球置于掌心向上抛起，同时右臂略外旋，拍面后仰角度较小，向右后上方引拍。当球从高点下降至稍高于网或与网同高时，前臂向前为主，向下为辅用力，以球拍中上部偏左的地方触球，减少向下摩擦球的力量，近似将

6. No-spin serve

(1) When doing the no-spin serve with the forehand, your body position should be the same as that for the forehand backspin serves. Use the left hand to hold the ball in the palm and throw it up; at the same time slightly turn the right arm outwards and tilt the racket face backward with a smaller angle, swinging the racket back toward the upper-right back direction. When the ball falls to the height that is a little higher than the net or to the same height with the net, the forearm should primarily put strength forward and assistantly downward. You should use the place which deflects to the left of the middle-upper part on the racket to contact the ball, reducing the downward friction force to the ball

球向前推出，使作用力接近球心，从而形成不转球。击球后，手臂随势向前挥动，身体重心移至左脚。

（2）反手发不转球时，站位同反手发下旋球。左手持球置于掌心向上抛起，同时右臂向左后上方引拍，当球从高点下降至稍高于球网或与网同高时，以较小的手臂内旋幅度和较小的拍面后仰角度，用球拍的中上部触球的中部或中部偏下，减小向下摩擦球的力量，近似将球推出，使作用力接近球心。击球后，手臂随势向右前方挥动。身体重心移至右脚。不转发球要与加转发球结合使用才会获得好的效果。在发球时关键是球拍不要太后仰，用球拍的中上部触球，用力方向以向前撞击为主，向下摩擦为辅，击球部位靠近中部或中部偏下，从而形成不转球。

and approximately pushing the ball forward. In the meantime make the applied force close to the center of the ball, thereby making the no-spin serve. After hitting the ball, the arm and hand should continue to swing forward along with the inertia, and the center of body weight should be shifted onto the left foot.

(2) When doing the no-spin serve with the backhand, your body position should be the same as that for the backhand backspin serves. Use the left hand to hold the ball in the palm and throw it up; in the meanwhile the right arm should swing the racket back toward the upper-left back direction. When the ball falls from the peak to the height that is a little higher than the net or to the same height with the net, turn the arm and hand inward in a smaller range with the racket face tilted backward slightly. And contact the middle or middle-lower part of the ball with the middle-upper part of the racket, reducing the downward friction force to ball, which is similar to pushing the ball forward; in the meantime make the applied force close to the center of the ball. After hitting the ball, the arm and hand should swing toward the right front along with the inertia, and the center of body weight should be shifted onto the right foot. The no-spin serve should be used in combination with the heavy-spin serve, and in this way it can obtain a good effect. When doing the serve, the key is that you should not tilt the racket backward too much. What is more, you should use the middle-upper part of the racket to contact the ball. For the direction of exertion, you should strike the ball forward primarily and downward assistantly. The hitting spot on the ball should be close to the middle or middle-lower part of it, which will make a no-spin serve.

7. 发侧上旋球

（1）正手发左侧上旋球：左侧上旋球旋转力较强，对方挡球时向其右侧上方反弹，一般站在中线偏左或侧身发球。击球前，站位左半台，左脚在前，右脚在后。左手持球置于掌心向上抛起，同时向右上方引拍，腰部略向右转动。横握拍者手腕外展，使拍面方向略偏向左侧。当球从高点下降至接近网高时，右臂从右上方向左下方挥动，球拍从球的右侧中下部向左侧面摩擦，并微微勾手腕以加强上旋。击球后，前臂加速向左方挥摆，直握拍者手腕作屈，横握拍者手腕内收，配合腰部左转。（如图3-23）

7. Side topspin serve

(1) Forehand left-side topspin serve: the left-side topspin serve has a strong rotary force, when an opponent blocks the ball, it will rebound toward his (or her) upper-right direction. When doing the forehand left-side topspin serve, generally you should stand on the left of the center line or adopt sideways service. Before hitting the ball, your body position should be at the left half of the table with the left foot in the front and the right foot in the back. The left hand holds the ball in the palm and throws it up. Simultaneously, you should swing the racket backward toward the upper-right direction turning your waist slightly to the right. For the players of shake-hand grip, the wrist should slightly abduct to make the direction of the racket face deflect to the left side. When the ball falls from the peak to around the same height with the net, the right arm should swing from the upper right to the lower left. Make the racket graze the ball from its middle-lower part of the right side to the left side and bend the wrist slightly to strengthen topspin. After hitting the ball, the forearm should speed up to swing toward the left. For the players of pen-hold grip, the wrist should bend; and for the players of shake-hand grip, the wrist should retract inwards; in the same time cooperate to rotate the waist to the left. (As shown in fig.3-23)

1　　　　2　　　　3　　　　4

图3-23　正手发左侧上旋球

Fig.3-23　Forehand left-side topspin serve

（2）反手发右侧上旋球：发球员在身体的反手位由左向右挥拍摩擦，球速较慢，但右侧上旋转力较强。对方平挡回接时，球向发球员的右侧上方（即接球员的左侧上方）飞出。

击球前，站位左半台，离台约30厘米，右脚稍前，重心在右脚上，球与拍均置于身体左侧，抛球同时向左转腰引拍至左后上方，手腕内屈，使拍面朝左上方。击球时，当球下落时手臂自左上方向右下方挥摆，触球时拍面从球的中下部向左侧上部摩擦。击球后，腰配合向右转动，手臂从左后上方向右前上方顺势挥动。（如图3-24）

（2）Backhand right-side topspin serve: the server should be in the backhand position of the body and swing the racket to graze the ball from left to right. The right-side topspin serve has relatively slow ball speed but its rotating force is rather strong. When an opponent blocks the ball to return, it will fly off toward the upper right side of the server (namely, the upper left side of the receiver).

Before hitting the ball, your body position should be at the left half of the table, about 30 cm from it with the right foot a little bit in the front, and the center of body weight on the right foot. Put both the ball and racket in the left side of the body. While throwing the ball, rotate the waist to the left and swing the racket back toward the upper-left back direction, with the wrist bended inward to make the racket face toward the upper left. For hitting the ball, when the ball is falling, the racket hand and arm swing from the upper left toward the lower right. When contacting the ball, you should make the racket graze it from its middle-lower part toward the upper part of the left side. After hitting the ball, rotate the waist to the right in cooperation; and the hand and arm should swing from the upper-left back direction toward the upper-right front direction along with the inertia. (As shown in fig.3-24)

图3-24 反手发右侧上旋球
Fig.3-24 Backhand right-side topspin serve

8. 发侧下旋球

（1）正手发左侧下旋球：左侧下旋球旋转力较强，对方挡球时，向其右侧下方反弹，一般站在中线偏左或侧身发球。

击球前，一般站位左半台，左手掌心托球置于身体右侧方。引拍时，左手将球向上抛起，同时右臂外旋，直握拍手腕弯曲，横握拍手腕外展，使拍面方向略偏向左侧，向右上方引拍，腰部略向右转动。击球时，当球从高点下降至接近网高时，手臂自右上方向左前下方挥出摆动，球拍从球的右侧中下部向左侧下部摩擦。击球后，腰配合向左转动，右臂从右上方向左下方顺势挥动。（如图3-25）

8. Side backspin serve

(1) Forehand left-side backspin serve: the left-side backspin serve has a strong rotary force; when an opponent blocks the ball, it will rebound toward his (or her) lower-right direction. Generally, you should stand on the left of the center line or adopt sideways service.

Before hitting the ball, your body position should be at the left half of the table; and hold the ball on the palm of the left hand which should be placed on the right side of the body. When swinging the racket back, the left hand should throw the ball up at the same time the right arm should turn outward. For players of the pen-hold grip, the wrist should do a bending motion; and for players of shake-hand grip, the wrist should abduct to make the racket face slightly deflect to the left side. You should swing the racket back toward the upper-right direction turning the waist slightly to the right. For hitting the ball, when the ball falls from the peak to around the same height with the net, the right arm should swing from the upper right to the lower-left front direction making the racket graze the ball from the middle-lower part of its right side to the lower part of the left side. After hitting the ball, rotate the waist to the left in cooperation; and the right arm should swing from the upper right toward the lower left along with the inertia. (As shown in fig.3-25)

图 3-25　正手发左侧下旋球

Fig.3-25　Forehand left-side backspin serve

（2）反手发右侧下旋球：球的飞行弧线向对方左侧偏拐，对方用平挡回球时，球向其左侧下方反弹。

击球前，站左半台，离台约 30 厘米，右脚稍前，球与拍均置于身体左侧。向左转腰，球抛起，快速向左后上方引拍至左肘下方外侧处，手腕内屈，使拍面朝左上方。当球下落时，手臂自左后上方向右前下方挥动出摆，触球时，拍面从球的左侧中下部向右侧摩擦。

击球后，腰配合向右转动，手臂从左后上方向右前下方挥动。（如图 3-26）

(2) Backhand right-side backspin serve: the flying trajectory of the ball will deflect to the left side of an opponent; when an opponent blocks the ball, it will rebound toward his (or her) lower-left direction.

Before hitting the ball, your body position should be at the left half of the table, about 30 cm from it with the right foot a little in the front, and you should place both the ball and the racket on the left side of the body. Rotate the waist to the left throwing up the ball; and swing back the racket quickly toward the upper-left back direction until it gets to the place which is below and outside the left elbow, with the wrist bended inward to make the racket face toward the upper left. When the ball is falling, the arm and hand should swing from the upper-left back direction to the lower-right front direction. When contacting the ball, you should make the racket graze it from the middle-lower part of its left side to the right side.

After hitting the ball, rotate the waist to the right in cooperation; and the hand and arm should swing from the upper-left back toward the lower-right front direction. (As shown in fig.3-26)

图 3-26 反手发右侧下旋球
Fig.3-26 Backhand right-side backspin serve

9. 下蹲式发球

击球前的准备（包括站位，抛球引拍）：左脚稍前，身体略向右偏转，左手掌心托球置于身体右前方，左手将球向上抛起，同时做下蹲姿势，右臂上举比肩高，引拍路线最好呈半弧状，手腕外展，拍面方向略向后仰。

击球时，当球从高点下降至约网高时，前臂加速从左向右前方挥动，手腕同时做内收，击球中部向右侧上部摩擦。这样发出的是正手右侧上旋球（如图 3-27）。如果击球中下部向右下方摩擦，则可以发出右侧下旋球（如图 3-28）。

击球后，手臂继续向右前方挥动并迅速还原。

9. Squatting serve

Preparations before hitting the ball (including the stance, throwing the ball and backswing of the racket): put the left foot slightly in the front with the body turned a little bit to the right. Hold the ball on the palm of the left hand which should be placed on the right-front side of the body. Then throw up the ball with the left hand in the meantime, perform a squatting posture, lifting the right arm over the shoulder; and you'd better shape the line of racket backswing as a half arc, abducting the wrist with the racket face slightly tilted backward.

For hitting the ball, when the ball falls from the peak to around the same height with the net, the forearm should speed up to swing from the left to the right front direction; at the same time, the wrist should do an adducting motion, with the racket hitting the middle part of the ball and graze it toward the upper part of the right side. In this way the serve is the forehand right-side topspin. (As shown in fig.3-27) If you hits the middle-lower part of the ball and graze it toward the lower right, you can serve the right-side backspin. (As shown in fig.3-28)

After hitting the ball, the arm and hand should continue to swing toward the right front and quickly recover.

1　　　2　　　3　　　4

图 3-27 下蹲式右侧上旋球
Fig.3-27　Right-side topspin squatting serve

图 3-28　下蹲式右侧下旋球
Fig.3-28　Right-side backspin squatting serve

10. 逆旋转发球

逆旋转发球是近些年世界乒坛流行的技术，它能够丰富发球的旋转变化，其动作隐蔽，出手迅速，发力协调，旋转较强。

（1）发逆旋转上旋球动作要点：击球前，左脚在前，右脚稍后，抛球最好往怀内抛一点，引拍后肘部抬起，球拍引到腋下附近。击球时，肘部像一个支点，触球左侧上部，向前用力。拍面通过手腕内勾外撇控制，有种剐蹭球的感觉。击球后，前臂有种向前顶出、铲出的感觉。（如图 3-29）

10. Reverse-spin serve

The reverse-spin serve is a popular technique in the world table tennis in recent years which is able to enrich the changes of spin for serves. It is hidden and quick in action and can give force harmonically with stronger spin.

(1) Movement essentials for the reverse-topspin serve: before hitting the ball, you should put the left foot in the front and the right foot slightly in the back. When throwing the ball, you'd better throw it a little inward the bosom. After swinging the racket back, you should lift the elbow to bring the racket near to armpit. When hitting the ball, you should take the elbow as a pivot and put forth your strength forward, contacting the upper part on the left side of the ball; and incurve and outcurve your wrist to control the racket face with a feeling of cutting and rubbing the ball. After hitting the ball, there is a feeling that you move the forearm forward to push and shovel the ball out. (As shown in fig.3-29)

图 3-29 逆旋转上旋球
Fig.3-29 Reverse-topspin serve

（2）发逆旋转下旋球动作要点：击球前，左脚在前，右脚稍后，抛球最好往怀内抛一点，引拍后肘部抬起，球拍引到腋下附近。击球时，肘部像一个支点，触球的中下部，向下发力。击球后，前臂有种向前顶出、铲出的感觉。（如图 3-30）

(2) Movement essentials for the reverse-backspin serve: before hitting the ball, you should put the left foot in the front and the right foot slightly in the back. When throwing the ball, you'd better throw it a little inward the bosom. After swinging the racket back, you should lift the elbow to bring the racket near to armpit. When hitting the ball, you should take the elbow as a pivot and put forth your strength downward, contacting the middle-lower part of the ball. After hitting the ball, there is a feeling that you move the forearm forward to push and shovel the ball out. (As shown in fig.3-30)

图 3-30 逆旋转下旋球
Fig.3-30 Reverse-backspin serve

11. 正手高抛发球

（1）特点：最显著的特点是抛球高，增大了球下降时对拍的正压力，发出的球速度快、冲力大、旋转变化多，着台后拐弯飞行。但高抛发球动作复杂，有一定的难度。

11. Forehand high-toss serve

(1) Characteristics: the most conspicuous characteristic is that throwing the ball high increases the positive pressure of the ball to the racket when it goes down, which makes the ball served with fast speed, big impulsive force and more changes of spin. When the ball touches on the table, it will turn and fly away. But the high-toss serve has the certain difficulty due to the complicated action.

（2）发球要点：左脚稍前，两脚分开，与肩同宽，身体与球台端线约成60°角，抛球前持球手臂稍贴身体，稍收腹，球置于掌心，两膝微屈；抛球时，手腕固定，前臂平稳向上直抛，腰和膝同时顺势向上挺伸，重心在左脚上，同时，向右后上方引拍，手腕充分外展；挥拍击球时，球拍从右后上方向左前方快速摆动，腕关节内收发力，腰向左转配合用力。(如图3-31)

(2) Serve essentials: you should put the left foot in the front slightly with the two feet a shoulder-width apart and about a 60° angle between your body and the end line of the table. Before throwing the ball, put the arm which holds the ball slightly close to your body; meanwhile, draw the abdomen in and hold the ball in the palm, with both knees bending a bit. When throwing the ball, use the forearm to throw it steady straight upward with the wrist immobilized; and the waist and knees conveniently stretch upwards at one time, with the center of body weight on the left foot. At the same time swing the racket back toward the upper-right back direction and fully abduct the wrist. When swinging the racket to hit the ball, you should swing the racket from the upper-right back direction toward the left-front direction and retract the wrist joint inwards to put forth your strength; in the meantime, rotate the waist to the left to give force coordinately. (As shown in fig.3-31)

图 3-31 正手高抛发球

Fig.3-31 Forehand high-toss serve

12. 发球的练习方法：

（1）单一线路练习，先斜线，后直线，再斜线、直线结合。

（2）单一旋转固定线路、定点练习。

（3）向特定的区域发球练习。（如图 3-32）

12. Training methods for serves:

(1) Single-line practice: first, practice the crosscourt serve, next, practice serving in the straight line; then practice the crosscourt serve in combination with the straight line serve.

(2) Practice single-spin serves for the fixed line and fixed point.

(3) Practice serving toward specific areas. (As shown in fig.3-32)

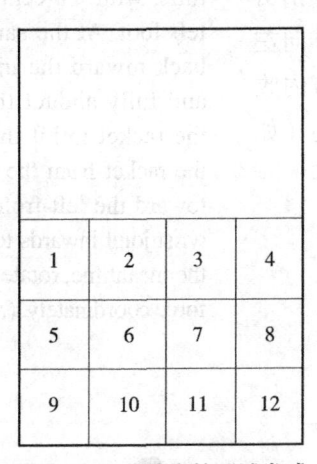

1	2	3	4
5	6	7	8
9	10	11	12

图 3-32　向特定的区域发球

Fig.3-32　Serve to the specific areas

（4）单一旋转不定线路、不定点练习。

（5）发球速度先慢后快练习。

（6）先低抛再高抛练习。

（7）用相似手法练习两种不同旋转、不同落点的发球。

(4) Practice single-spin serves for the unfixed line and unfixed point.

(5) First practice serving at a slow speed, then serve at a fast speed.

(6) First practice throwing the ball lowly, then throw it highly.

(7) Practice performing two serves of different rotating directions and different placements with a similar technique.

第五节
接发球技术

在乒乓球比赛中，接发球的机会与发球大致相同，如接发球不好，除直接失分外，还会影响自己的战术发挥，造成心理压力而处于被动。因此，必须掌握好接发球技术。要想接好发球，首先必须对发球的旋转、落点等变化做出正确的判断，并根据自己的技术特长，果断、合理地运用接发球技术，以摆脱被动局面，取得主动。

1. 接发球的基本技术

首先，要减少接发球的直接失误，在此基础上提高接发球的质量。另外，不要始终用一种方式接同一发球，否则对方容易适应。要积极主动抢攻，克服单纯求稳的思想。

（1）接发球的判断。

①就对方发球时的站位决定自己接发球的站位。如对方位于右角用正手发球时，接球者应站在中线偏右处；发球者位于正手位侧身发球时，接发者应站在中线偏左处。

Section 5
Receiving techniques

In table tennis matches, the chances of receiving and serving are roughly the same. If you cannot receive a serve well, in addition to direct score loss, it will affect your tactical play and cause the psychological pressure to you and throw you into a passive position. So, you must master receiving techniques well. If you want to return a serve well, first of all, you must make the accurate judgment for the change of spin and placement of the ball served. Then you should use the receiving techniques decisively and reasonably according to your own technique specialty, thereby get rid of the passive situation to gain the initiative.

1. Basic techniques of receiving

Firstly, you should reduce the direct fault of receiving serves and improve the quality of receiving serves on this basis. Moreover, you should not return serves of the same kind in a single way all the time or else it is easy for your opponent to adapt to it. You should be proactive and take the initiative to attack, overcoming the thought which demands stability merely.

(1) Judgment for receiving.

①You should decide your position of receiving according to the opponent's position while you is serving. When the opponent stands at the right corner to serve with the forehand, the receiver should stand in the position which is slightly off to the right of the center line. When the opponent

②观察对方发球前的引拍方向。例如，发下旋球，球拍向上引；发左侧旋球，球拍向右引。

③观察球拍触球瞬间摩擦球的方向，判断球的旋转性质。例如，球拍由上向下切球，为下旋；由左向右摩擦球，为右侧旋等。

④根据发球的第一落点判断来球的长短。发球的第一落点靠近发球方端线一般是长球，靠近球网是短球。

（2）接发球的具体技术运用。

①接上旋球（奔球）：用正、反手攻球，快带技术或（直拍）推挡回接，拍面适当前倾，击球的中上部，调节好向前的力量。

②接下旋长球：用搓球、削球或提拉球回接，搓或削时多向前用力。

does sideways service in the forehand position, the receiver should stand in the position which is slightly off to the left of the center line.

② You should observe the direction of the racket backswing of the opponent before a serve. For example, if he(or she) is going to make the backspin serve, he(or she) swings the racket backward and upward; if he(or she) is going to make the left-side spin serve, he (or her) swings the racket back toward the right.

③ You should observe the direction of grazing the ball by the racket in the instant when the racket contacts the ball, thereby judge the spinning nature of the ball. For example, if the racket cuts the ball from up to down, the serve is backspin; if the racket grazes the ball from left to right, the serve is right-side spin, etc.

④ You should judge whether the oncoming ball is long or short according to the first placement of the serve. Generally if the first placement of the serve is close to the end line of the serving side, the oncoming ball is long; if the first placement of the serve is close to the net, the oncoming ball is short.

(2) The specific technique application for receiving.

① Returning the topspin serve (the deep topspin serve): You should return the topspin serve with the forehand and backhand attack, the technique of fast block or block (pen-hold grip); and appropriately tilt the racket face forward to hit the middle-upper part of the ball, adjusting the forward force well.

② Returning the long backspin serve: You should return the long backspin serve with push, chop or the topspin lift. When returning the serve with push or chop, you should put

③接左侧上（下）旋球：可采用攻球、快拨技术或推挡（搓球或拉球）回接，拍面稍前倾（后仰）并略向左偏斜，击球偏右中上（中下）部，以抵消来球的左侧上（下）旋力。

④接右侧上（下）旋球：可采用攻球、快拨技术或推挡（搓球或拉球）回接，拍面稍前倾（后仰）并略向右偏斜，击球偏左中上（中下）部；回接要点和方法与接左侧上（下）旋球相同。

⑤接近网短球：用快搓或台内拧拉或挑打技术突击回接，主要靠手腕和前臂的力量。

⑥接转与不转球：在判断不准的情况下，可轻轻地托一板或撇一板，但要注意弧线和落点。

⑦接高抛发球：如球着台后拐弯的程度大，应向拐弯方向提前引拍。

2. 接发球的练习方法

接发球技术能力的高

forth your strength forward more.

③Returning the left-side topspin (backspin) serve: You can use the drive and the fast block or block (push or the topspin lift) to return the serves with the racket face tilted slightly forward (or backward) and slightly deflected to the left, hitting the right middle-upper part (or the right middle-lower part) of the ball to counteract the left-side topspin (backspin) force of the oncoming ball.

④Returning the right-side topspin (backspin) serve: You can use the drive and the fast block or block (push or the topspin lift) to return the serves with the racket face tilted slightly forward (or backward) and slightly deflected to the right, hitting the left middle-upper part (or the left middle-lower part) of the ball. The essentials and methods of returning the serves are the same as that of the left-side topspin (backspin) serve.

⑤Returning the short serve: You can make aggressive return to the short serve with the techniques of the fast push and the over-the-table twist drive or the flip, mainly depending on the strength of the wrist and forearm.

⑥Returning the spin and no-spin serves: In the case that you cannot make a correct judgment for the serve, you can gently carry the ball forward or graze it from one side to the lower front of the other side; but you should beware of the trajectory and placement.

⑦ Returning the high-toss serve: If the ball bends to a large degree after it touches the table, you should swing the racket back toward the direction of bending in advance.

2. Training methods of receiving

The high and low technical capability of

低，常由其所掌握的基本技术的好坏所决定。因此，对初学者来说，要练好接发球技术，必须首先掌握乒乓球的各种基本技术。其练习方法和步骤如下：

（1）用快带、推、搓、削、拉中的任何一种技术去接对方的单一发球。

（2）先练习接上旋球，再练习接下旋球，最后练习接侧旋球。

（3）用一种技术接一种发球，如用搓球接下旋球、用推挡接上旋球。

（4）在限定的区域接球，提高控制能力。

（5）练习接侧上（下）旋球的技术，以适应不同旋转的变化。如接左（右）侧上（下）旋球时，要在对方拍触球的瞬间观察球的移动方向，来提高判断旋转的能力。

（6）在上述基础上，应进一步练习控制回球落点，以避免在接球后给对方带来较多的攻击机会。

（7）在有了较好的适应能力并能较较自如地控制回球落点之后，应逐步提高防

receiving serves is usually determined by the stand or fall of the basic techniques you has mastered. Therefore for beginners, if you want to practice the techniques of receiving well, you must first master all kinds of basic techniques of table tennis. The training methods and procedures are as follows:

(1) You can use any kind of techniques among the fast block, block, push, chop and the topspin lift to return the single kind of serves by the other person involved.

(2) Practice receiving the topspin serve first, then practice receiving the backspin serve; last practice returning the side-spin serve.

(3) Receive one kind of serve with a single technique; for example, to return the backspin serve with push and return the topspin serve with block.

(4) Return serves toward the specific areas to improve the ability of control.

(5) Practice the receiving technique for the side topspin (backspin) to adapt to the different spins. For example, when receiving the left-side (the right-side) topspin (backspin) serves, in the instant of the opponent's racket contacting the ball you should observe the movement direction of the ball to improve the ability of judgment for spins.

(6) On the basis of the above, you should further practice controlling the placement of returning the ball in order to avoid giving the opponent more attacking opportunities after your returning.

(7) After you have good adaptability to return serves and can control the placement of the returning ball more freely, you should gradually increase the defense ability for the

御对方抢攻的本领。接球后应能顶住对方抢攻。回球应有落点变化，能把球回到对方空当，以避免受到对方连续攻击。

（8）当接发球防御有一定基础后，就可以开始练习拉球或抢攻的接发球技术。其顺序也应是从接单一发球到接配套发球，从固定落点到不固定落点，从采用一种接法到结合多种接法。这样由浅入深，循序渐进使之逐渐和实战密切结合起来，提高接发球技术水平。

第六节
攻球技术

攻球是乒乓球比赛中争取主动和获得胜利的重要技术，具有快速、有力的特点。它既是初学者必须掌握的主要技术，又是各种类型的打法和各种战术组成的基础。

1. 正手近台攻球

正手近台攻球又称正手快攻。它具有站位近，动作

preemptive attack by your opponent. You should be able to resist the preemptive attack by the opponent after returning a serve; and return serves with the change of placement. You should be able to return a serve to the empty position of your opponent in order to avoid suffering continuous attacks from the opponent.

(8) After having a considerable basis in the defense for serve receiving, you can start practicing to return the served ball with the techniques of the topspin lift or the preemptive attack. The order should be from receiving one kind of serve to returning a complete set of serves, from returning the served ball to the fixed placement to returning it to the unfixed placement; and from using one kind of receiving technique to applying a variety of receiving techniques in combination. You should do in this way from the easy to the difficult and complicated step by step making it gradually and closely combined with actual combat to raise the level of receiving techniques.

Section 6
Attacking techniques

In a table tennis match, attack is the important technique to gain the initiative and win the game, which has the characteristics of high speed and great force. It is the main technique a beginner must master and the basis of various types of play and all kinds of tactic composition as well.

1. Close-table forehand attack

The close-table forehand attack is also known as the forehand fast drive, which has the

小，速度快的特点。在比赛中，可直接得分或在相持中结合落点变化，调动对方。

击球前，左脚稍前，右脚稍后，身体离台约50厘米，手臂自然放松，保持一定弯曲。随着身体转动，手臂向身体右后侧方引拍。击球时，当来球弹起时，手臂迅速向左前上方挥动（肘部不要夹得太紧，手臂要呈半圆形挥动），在球的上升期击球的中上部（直握拍者击球时，拇指压拍，食指放松，拍面前倾，结合手腕内转发力动作）。同时身体重心由右脚移至左脚。击球后，迅速还原，准备下板击球。（如图3-33）

characteristics of close-to-table position, small action and fast speed. In the match you can use it to score directly or move your opponent in combination with the placement change in a stalemate.

Before hitting the ball, put the left foot a little bit in the front and the right foot slightly in the back with the body about 50 cm from the table; and relax the arms and hands which should be kept with certain bending. As the body turns, the racket hand and arm swing the racket back toward the right back side of the body. For hitting the ball, when the ball bouncing up you should swing the racket hand and arm quickly toward the upper-left front direction (the elbow cannot clip too tight; the arm swings as a semicircle), and hit the middle-upper part of the ball at its ascending stage (when hitting the ball, pen-holders should use the thumb to press the racket relaxing the forefinger with the racket face tilted forward, and turn the wrist inward to give force in combination). At the same time transfer the center of body weight from the right foot to the left foot. After hitting the ball, recover quickly and get ready for the next shot. (As shown in fig.3-33)

1　　　　2　　　　3　　　　4

a. 横拍正手近台攻球

a. Close-table forehand attack with shake-hand grip

b. 直拍正手近台攻球
b.Close-table forehand attack with pen-hold grip

图 3-33　正手近台攻球
Fig.3-33　Close-table forehand attack

2. 正手中远台攻球

正手中台攻球站位离台稍远，动作幅度大，力量大。常在对攻或在防御反击时使用。击球前，身体向右转动，增大向右后引拍的幅度，重心在右脚上；击球时，用力蹬地，转腰，上臂带动前臂和手腕向左前上方发力，击球点离身体稍远一点，在来球下降前期击球的中部或稍偏下，并向上摩擦；击球后，上臂带动前臂，并借助蹬地和转腰的力量，使身体重心移至左脚。（如图 3-34）

2. Middle and back court forehand attack

For the middle and back court forehand attack, which has a large range of movement and great force, your body position should be farther from the table. It is often used in counter drives or in the defensive counter attack. Before hitting the ball, turn your body to the right to increase the backswing range of the racket toward the right back direction with the center of body weight on the right foot. When hitting the ball, you should thrust against the ground forcefully and rotate your waist with the upper arm driving the forearm and wrist to put forth strength toward the upper-left front direction. The hitting point should have a little distance away from the body; and additionally, you should hit the middle part or slightly lower on the oncoming ball at its early descending stage and graze it upward. After hitting the ball, you should use the upper arm to drive the forearm with the aid of the power produced by thrusting against the ground and turning the waist, and move the center of body weight to the left foot. (As shown in fig.3-34)

1　　　　　　　2　　　　　　　3　　　　　　　4

a. 横拍正手中远台攻球

a. Middle and back court forehand attack with shake-hand grip

1　　　　　　　2　　　　　　　3　　　　　　　4

b. 直拍正手中远台攻球

b. Middle and back court forehand attack with pen-hold grip

图 3-34　正手中远台攻球

Fig.3-34　Middle and back court forehand attack

3. 正手扣杀高球

击球前左脚稍前，右脚稍后，站位远近根据来球长短而定。手臂随着腰和髋向右后方转动，整个手臂后拉，将球拍引至身体右后上方，适当加大引拍距离，便于加速和发力。

3. Forehand smash against a lob

Before hitting the ball, put the left foot a little bit in the front and the right foot slightly in the back. The distance between your position and the table should be determined in accordance with the length of the oncoming ball. Turn the arm and hand toward the right back direction along with the waist and hips; and swing the

击球时，当来球跳至高点期，拍面前倾，击球的中上部，上臂带动前臂同时加速向左前下方发力挥动，同时配合腰部转动及蹬地的力量。来球不转或带上旋时，球拍位置应略高于来球。击球后，手臂随势向左前下方挥动并迅速还原。（如图3-35）

entire arm backward bringing the racket to the upper-right back direction of the body. You should appropriately increase the backswing distance of the racket so as to accelerate and give force. For hitting the ball, when the oncoming ball bounces to the peak stage you should hit the middle-upper part of the ball with the racket face tilted forward (closed racket face) and the upper arm driving the forearm to accelerate and swing simultaneously toward the lower-left front direction, at the same time cooperating with the force produced by thrusting against the ground and turning the waist. If the oncoming ball is no-spin or topspin, the racket position should be slightly higher than the ball. After hitting the ball, the arm and hand should swing toward the lower-left front direction along with the inertia and quickly recover. (As shown in fig.3-35)

a. 横拍正手扣杀高球
a. Shake-hand grip forehand smash against a lob

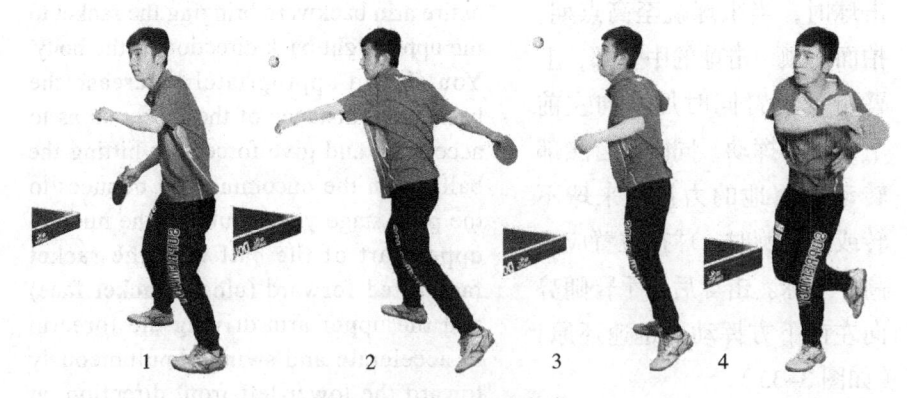

1　　　　　　　2　　　　　　　3　　　　　　　4

b. 直拍正手扣杀高球

c. Pen-hold grip forehand smash against a lob

图 3-35　正手扣杀高球

Fig.3-35　Forehand smash against a lob

4. 正手挑打

正手挑打是用于攻击台内近网短球的技术。具有动作小，出手突然，主动意识强的特点。

击球前，右腿插入球台内部，前臂自然弯曲，拍面向来球中下部插入。

击球时，上身前倾，转动手腕，触球中部或中上部，略带摩擦。前臂快速收缩，动作幅度小，靠手腕爆发力将球击出。靠手腕变化控制拍形以及回球落点。击球后，右脚用力蹬地还原。

4. Forehand flip

The forehand flip is a technique used for attacking the near-net drop shot over the table, which has the characteristics of small actions, making moves suddenly and strongly active consciousness.

Before hitting the ball, insert the right leg under the table, and bend the forearm naturally to insert the racket face toward the middle-lower part of the oncoming ball.

When hitting the ball, you should bend the upper body forward and turn the wrist, contacting the middle or middle-upper part of the ball with a slight friction; and contract the forearm rapidly and hit the ball out by the explosive force of the wrist with small and skillful movement range. In the meantime, you should control the racket angle and the placement of return by changes of the wrist. After hitting the ball, the right foot should thrust against the ground forcibly to recover.

挑打上旋来球，触球中上部，拍面稍前倾，略带摩擦，前臂收缩幅度不能过大，否则容易造成回球出界。要依靠手腕的力量击球，手腕尽量向前运动。

When flipping the oncoming ball of topspin, you should contact the middle-upper part of it and tilt the racket slightly forward with a slight friction. The contraction range of the forearm should be not too much; otherwise it is prone to cause the ball outside. You must rely on the strength of the wrist to hit the ball and make the wrist move forward as far as possible.

挑打下旋来球，触球中部，靠前臂以及手腕向前上方运动来加强摩擦。挑打后，右腿用力蹬地还原，以确保下一板球的衔接。（如图 3-36）

When flipping the oncoming ball of backspin, you should contact the middle part of it; at the same time strengthen the friction by moving the forearm and wrist forward and upward. After flipping the ball, the right leg should thrust against the ground forcibly to recover in order to ensure the link of the next shot. (As shown in fig.3-36)

a. 横拍正手挑打
a. Forehand flip with shake-hand grip

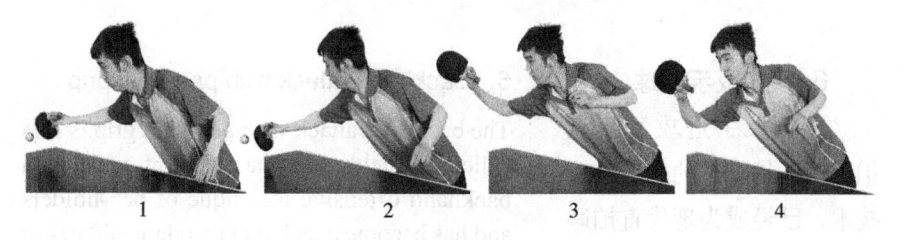

b. 直拍正手挑打
b. Forehand flip with pen-hold grip

图 3-36　正手挑打
Fig.3-36　Forehand flip

5. 横拍反手攻球

横拍反手攻球时，右脚稍前于左脚，身体稍向左偏斜，应先向左后方引拍，略收腹，拍面稍倾斜，在来球的上升期，击球的中上部，靠大臂带动小臂，适当借助腰腿的力量。手腕要控制好拍型。发力向右前上方挥拍，击球后迅速还原。（如图 3-37）

5. Backhand attack with shake-hand grip

When performing the backhand attack with shake-hand grip, put the right foot a little bit in the front to the left foot with the body slightly deflecting to the left. First, you should swing the racket back toward the left back direction and slightly draw the abdomen in, with racket face tilted a little bit. Hit middle-upper part of the oncoming ball at its ascending stage, and make the upper arm bring the forearm with the appropriate aid of the strength produced by the waist and legs. You should use the wrist to control the racket angle well and swing the racket forcefully toward the upper-right front direction. After hitting the ball recover quickly. (As shown in fig.3-37)

图 3-37　横拍反手攻球
Fig.3-37　Backhand attack with shake-hand grip

6. 直拍反手攻球

直拍反手进攻又叫直拍横打，是直拍的反面进攻技术，已经成为现代直拍运动员必须掌握的一项技术。直拍横打技术包括快拨、快带、挑打、弹击、拉球、反拉等。我们练习时可以从最简单的快拨开始，再练习快带和拉球等就比较容易了。

6. Backhand attack with pen-hold grip

The backhand attack with pen-hold grip is also called pen-held racket backside hit, which is a backhand offensive technique of pen-holders and has become a technique modern athletes of pen-hold grip must master. It includes the fast flick, the fast block, the flip, the snap, the loop drive and counter loop, etc. When practicing, you can start from the fast flick which is the most simple, then it is easier to practice the fast block and loop drive, etc.

要领：用直拍反面击球，站位离台40～50厘米，左脚稍前，收前臂于左腹前，身体重心稍下降，手腕内曲，前臂内旋，拍面前倾，在来球的上升期向右前上方击打，摩擦来球的中上部。（如图3-38）

Movement essentials: use the reverse side of a pen-held racket to hit the ball. Your position should be 40~50 cm from the table with the left foot slightly in the front. Draw the forearm in the front the left abdomen and lower the center of body weight slightly, with the wrist incurved and the forearm turned inward. You should tilt the racket face forward to hit the oncoming ball toward the upper-right front direction at its ascending stage grazing the middle-upper part of the ball. (As shown in fig.3-38)

图 3-38　直拍横打

Fig.3-38　Backhand attack with pen-hold grip

7. 攻球的练习方法

（1）原地徒手模仿练习，体会动作要领。

（2）结合步法做徒手练习。

（3）推攻练习：一人推挡一人练正手攻球或反手攻球，要求力量由小到中等，待稍熟练后再发力或快攻。练习形式有攻斜线、攻直线、攻中路，在

7. Training methods for attacking techniques

(1) Use the racket hand to imitate the movements of attacking on site without the ball, experiencing the movement essentials.

(2) Do the barehanded practice imitating the movements of attacking in combination with footwork.

(3) Do the block-attack practice. One player returns the ball with blocks and the other practices the forehand attack or the backhand attack, demanding the degree of force from small to medium. Do not give force or attack quickly until being more skilled. The training forms are attacking crosscourt, attacking

半台范围内或在三分之二球台范围内攻球。

（4）两点攻一点练习：要求推挡者把球推到攻球者两点，攻球者在移动中将球击到对方一个位置。开始练习时，两点角度变化小一些，然后逐渐增加。

（5）一点攻两点练习。

（6）正手斜线对攻、正手直线对攻、正手中路对攻练习。

（7）推挡侧身正手攻斜线练习。

（8）两人对推斜线，侧身攻直线练习。

（9）左推右攻练习。

（10）对搓中侧身抢拉或正手突击练习。

（11）用多球扣杀机会球或高球练习。

第七节
弧圈球技术

弧圈球是一种强烈的上旋球，具有稳健性高、

in straight lines, attacking to the middle, attacking within half a table or two-thirds of the table.

(4) Practice attacking from two positions to one position, which demands that the blocker return the ball to two positions for the attacker, who should hit back the ball in motion to one position of the opponent. At the beginning of the practice the blocker should change the angle between the two positions in a smaller range and then increase it gradually.

(5) Practice attacking from one position toward two positions.

(6) Practice forehand counter attacks crosscourt, forehand counter attacks in straight lines and forehand counter attacks to the middle.

(7) Both players block against block and then, the attacker should move sideways to attack crosscourt with the forehand.

(8) Both players block against block and then, the attacker should move sideways to attack in straight lines with the forehand.

(9) Practice backhand block with forehand attack.

(10) In counter pushes the attacker should move sideways to loop first or make a sudden attack with the forehand.

(11) Multi-ball practice for smashing against a chance ball or a lob.

Section 7
Loop drive techniques

The loop drive is a kind of strong topspin with the characteristics of high stability,

攻击力强、威力大的特点。它把速度和旋转有机地结合起来，形成了横拍、直拍多种弧圈球打法，是现代乒乓球运动中的一项重要技术。弧圈球的基本技术有如下几种。

1. 正手拉加转弧圈球（又称高吊弧圈球）

特点：上旋强烈、弧线高、运行速度较慢，但落台后向下滑落较快。对方回击易出高球，是对付削球、搓球和接出台下旋发球的有效技术。

击球前，右脚稍后，身体略右转，右肩略低，手腕外展，手臂自然下垂，向右后下方引拍。击球时右脚掌内侧蹬地，以腰带动上臂、前臂向前挥动，击球瞬间前臂迅速收缩，在下降期击球的中部或中上部，球拍触球后迅速转为向前上方的摩擦；击球后球拍随势至头前，重心从右脚移到左脚，并迅速还原。（如图 3-39）

strong assaulting force and great power. It has combined speed with spin organically forming a variety of loop drive plays for the shake-hand grip and the pen-hold grip, and is an important technique in the modern table tennis sport. Basic techniques of loop drive are as fallows.

1. Forehand heavy-spin loop (also known as high loop)

It is characterized by strong topspin, high trajectory and slower travelling speed. However, the looped ball will drop down quickly after it falls on the table, which will easily cause the opponent to return with high ball, therefore, it is an effective technique to cope with the chop, push and return the backspin serve which is off the table.

Before hitting the ball, you should put the right foot a little bit in the back and turn the body slightly to the right, meanwhile, lower the right shoulder somewhat with the wrist extended outward and the arms drooped naturally; and swing the racket back toward the lower-right back direction. When hitting the ball, you should use the inner side of the sole of right foot to thrust against the ground, with the waist driving the upper arm and forearm to swing forward. In the instant of hitting the ball, contract the forearm to hit the middle or middle-upper part of the ball at its descending stage. After contacting the ball, change the racket quickly to graze it forward and upward. After hitting the ball, swing the racket to the front of the head along with inertia shifting the center of body weight from the right foot onto the left foot, and quickly recover. (As shown in fig.3-39)

a. 横拍正手拉加转弧圈球
a.Forehand heavy-spin loop with shake-hand grip

b. 直拍正手拉加转弧圈球
b.Forehand heavy-spin loop with pen-hold grip

图 3-39　正手拉加转弧圈球
Fig.3-39　Forehand heavy-spin loop

2. 正手拉前冲弧圈球

特点：上旋强烈、弧线低、速度快、前冲力强，落台后弹起不高，急剧前冲，向下滑落，具有扣杀球的效果，是对付推挡、搓球、发球及中等力量攻球的重要技术。

2. Forehand accelerated loop

It is characterized by strong topspin, low trajectory, fast travelling speed and great forward momentum. After the looped ball falls onto the table it will not bounce high, but move sharp forward and drop down quickly with the effect of the smashed ball. So, it is a major technique to cope with the block, push, serve and attack of medium strength. Before hitting the ball, you should stand astride and put the left foot a little bit in the front with the center of body weight slightly higher than that for the heavy-spin loop. Swing the racket back to the right back making it with the same height to the oncoming ball or slightly lower than the ball.

击球前两脚分开站立，左脚稍前，身体重心比加转弧圈球时稍高。球拍引至右后方，与来球同高或稍低。击球时上臂带动前臂向左前方发力，在上升后期或高点期击球的中部或中上部，击球瞬间应先向前控球，再向前摩擦球。横拍选手的食指应有前甩动作，直拍选手的中指应有顶拍动作。击球后重心前移至左脚。（如图3-40）

When hitting the ball, you should use the upper arm to drive the forearm to put forth strength toward the left front, hitting the middle or middle-upper part of the ball at its late ascending stage or the peak stage. In the instant of hitting the ball, you should first control the ball forward and then graze the ball forward. For players of shake-hand grip, the forefinger should have an action of throwing forward; and for players of pen-hold grip, the middle finger should have an action of backing against the racket. After hitting the ball, shift the center of body weight forward onto the left foot. (As shown in fig.3-40)

a. 横拍正手拉前冲弧圈球
a. Forehand accelerated loop with shake-hand grip

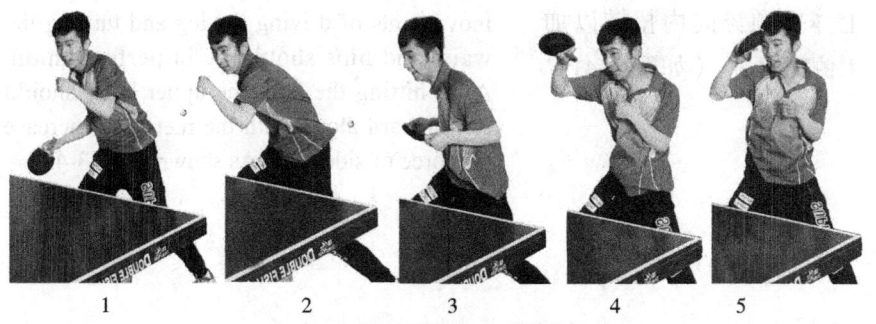

b. 直拍正手拉前冲弧圈球
b. Forehand accelerated loop with pen-hold grip

图 3-40　正手拉前冲弧圈球
Fig.3-40　Forehand accelerated loop

3. 正手拉侧旋弧圈球

侧旋弧圈球的飞行弧线一般比前冲弧圈球略高，比加转弧圈球低，落台后向右下方滑落，它可以加大拉球的角度，增加对方跑动范围和回球难度；同时这种技术还有变化节奏的作用。

击球前，两脚分开，两膝内收微曲。引拍位置略低于拉前冲弧圈球，手腕要放松。击球时，手臂自右外侧向左前上方（近似于弧形）发力。摩擦球的偏右面，拍形稍前倾。要求挥拍路线由后下方先向右侧前方，再向左前上方用力摩擦球，注意手腕要放松，蹬腿和转动腰髋动作协调一致。击球后，上体要顺势向内扭转以加大侧旋力量。（如图 3-41）

3. Forehand sidespin loop

Generally, the flying trajectory of the sidespin loop is a little higher than that of the accelerated loop and lower than that of the heavy-spin loop. After the looped ball falls onto the table it will drop down toward the lower-right direction, which can enlarge the angle of a loop drive, increasing the running range of an opponent, and making it more difficult to return. At the same time, this kind of technique in addition, has the function of changing the rhythm.

Before hitting the ball, you should stand astride with both knees inward retracted and slightly bent. The position of racket backswing should be somewhat lower than that for the accelerated loop, and the wrist should be relaxed. When hitting the ball, the arm and hand should put forth strength from the right outside toward the upper-left front direction (similar to an arc), grazing the ball by the right side with the racket angle tilted a little bit forward. For the path of swinging the racket, you should be required to swing it first from the lower back direction toward the right side of the front and then graze the ball forcefully toward the upper-left front direction. Pay attention, the wrist should be relaxed, the movements of driving the leg and turning the waist and hips should be in perfect union. After hitting the ball, the upper body should turn inward along with the inertia to increase the force of sidespin. (As shown in fig.3-41)

1　　　　2　　　　3　　　　4　　　　5

a. 横拍正手拉侧旋弧圈球

a.Forehand sidespin loop with shake–hand grip

1　　　　2　　　　3　　　　4　　　　5

b. 直拍正手拉侧旋弧圈球

b.Forehand sidespin loop with pen–hold grip

图 3-41　正手拉侧旋弧圈球

Fig.3-41　Forehand sidespin loop

4. 反手拉弧圈球

（1）横拍反手拉弧圈球。

其速度比正手拉弧圈球稍快，但力量和旋转略逊于正手。击球前两脚平行站立，略宽于肩，身体稍向左转，引拍动作为向左后方画一个小弧。击球时两脚蹬地，身体右转，前臂带动手腕向右前上方发力，击球的中部；触球后立即转为摩擦，用拇指

4. Backhand loop

(1) Backhand loop with shake-hand grip.

Its speed is a little faster than that of the forehand loop, but the strength and spin are slightly less than that of the forehand. Before hitting the ball, you should stand parallelly with a distance between the two feet slightly wider than the shoulder, and turn the body somewhat to the left. The movement of racket backswing is like drawing a small arc towards the left back direction. When hitting the ball, you should use your two feet to thrust against the ground and turn your body to the right with the forearm driving the wrist to put forth strength towards the upper-right front direction. You should hit the

调节击球的弧线。快拉时击球时间为上升前期；近台前冲时击球时间为上升后期或高点期；拉强烈加转或在中台向前上方发力拉时，击球时间为下降前期；中远台对拉的击球时间为下降中期。球出手后球拍随势至右肩前停止，然后迅速回归原位，准备下一板击球。（如图3-42）

middle part of the ball, and then immediately turn hitting into friction after contacting the ball with the thumb controlling the trajectory of hitting the ball. When performing the loop drive fast, hit the ball at its early ascending stage; when performing the accelerated loop in close-table positions, hit the ball at its late ascending stage or the peak stage; when performing the heavy-spin loop or looping forward and upward forcefully from the middle court, hit the ball at its early descending stage; when performing counter loop from the middle and back court, hit the ball in the middle of its descending stage. After the ball leaving off, swing the racket along with the inertia to stop at the front of the right shoulder; then quickly recover and get ready for the next stroke. (As shown in fig.3-42)

图 3-42　横拍反手拉弧圈球

Fig.3-42　Backhand loop with shake-hand grip

（2）直拍反手拉弧圈球。

特点与作用：拉球旋转较强，并带有上旋转性质，是直拍应对反手位下旋来球的有效进攻技术。

①直拍反面拉加转弧圈球（又称高吊弧圈）。

(2) Backhand loop with pen-hold grip.

Characteristics and functions: looping the ball with stronger spin and the properties of top spin, therefore, it is the effective technique for pen-holders to cope with an oncoming ball of backspin at the backhand location.

①Pen-held racket backside heavy-spin loop (also known as high loop).

击球前，身体重心略下沉。手腕自然下垂，但不要吊腕。

引拍时，腰部向左下方转动，以肘关节为轴，在球的下降前期击球，摩擦球的中下部。前臂、手腕朝上方摩擦，利用挺腹和两脚向上方的蹬力帮助发力，身体重心从左脚移至右脚。击球时主要用拇指和中指发力，食指自然放松。

②直拍反面拉前冲弧圈。

击球前，膝关节稍弯曲，收腹左脚可退半步，让出击球位置。身体重心比拉高吊弧圈略高一点。

击球时，前臂、手腕向前摩擦，最好拉球的上升期或高点期，击球的中上部，利用向前挺腹和两脚向前上方的蹬力辅助发力。（如图3-43）

Before hitting the ball, you should slightly lower down the center of body weight with the wrist drooped naturally, but do not hang down the wrist.

When swinging the racket back, rotate the waist to the lower left; and take the elbow joint as a pivot to graze the middle-lower part of the ball at its early descending stage. The forearm and wrist swing to graze the ball forward and upward. You should take advantage of erecting the stomach and the upward-push force by the two feet to put forth your strength, and in the meantime transfer the center of body weight from the left foot to the right foot. When hitting the ball, you should give force mainly by the thumb and middle finger with the forefinger relaxed naturally.

② Pen-held racket backside accelerated loop.

Before hitting the ball, you should bend the joints of the knees slightly with the abdomen drawn in; and you can move back the left foot for half a step to concede a place for hitting the ball, with the center of body weight slightly higher than that for the heavy-spin loop.

When hitting the ball, swing the forearm and wrist to graze the ball forward. It would be best to lift the ball at its ascending stage or the peak stage, hitting the middle-upper part of the ball. You should take advantage of erecting the stomach forward and the upward-push force by the two feet to help put forth your strength. (As shown in fig.3-43)

图 3-43 直拍反手拉弧圈球
Fig.3-43 Pen-held racket backside loop drive

（3）反手台内拧拉。

反手台内拧拉，即用反手拉正手位（或中路偏正手位）台内侧短球。充分摩擦球，容易克服来球旋转，可使回球稳定性好并且带有强烈旋转，从而在接发球过程中变被动为主动。

击球前，小幅上步，将重心压向右腿，身体几乎与球台端线平行。引拍时前臂与来球要保持适当距离，确保抓住最佳击球点，手腕内收幅度较大，收腹动作必须充分，给手臂动作让出足够空间。同时大臂向前上方抬起，前臂和手腕内收。

击球时，在来球的上升后期或最高点击球，提高回

(3) Backhand over-the-table twist drive.

The backhand over-the-table twist drive means to loop a short ball inside the playing surface with backhand at the forehand location (or the middle route near the forehand location). It hits the ball with full friction, which makes it easy to overcome the spinning of an oncoming ball in the meantime, can make good stability for returning the ball and a strong spinning thereby change a passive situation to an active situation in the process of receiving a serve.

Before hitting the ball, you should make a small step forward and shift the center of body weight to the right leg with the body almost parallel to the end line of the table. When swinging the racket back, you should keep a proper distance between the forearm and the oncoming ball insuring to catch hold of the optimal hitting point. You should retract the wrist inwards drastically and fully draw the abdomen in to make enough space for the movement of the arm. At the same time, raise the upper arm toward the upper front and retract the forearm and wrist inwards.

When hitting the ball, you should strike the oncoming ball at its late ascending stage or

球的威胁性。前臂以肘部为轴向右前方展开，整个手臂几乎伸直。手腕向外侧展开，要有爆发力。重心压向右腿，右腿弯曲。上半身始终保持前倾。（如图 3-44）

the peak stage to increase the threat of the returning and unfold the forearm toward the right front taking the elbow as a pivot; and what is more, you should almost straighten the entire arm. You must extend the wrist outwards with an explosive force. Put the center of body weight to the right leg which should be bent; and keep the upper part of the body leant forward from beginning to end. (As shown in fig.3-44)

a. 横拍反手台内拧拉
a. Backhand over-the-table twist drive with shake-hand grip

b. 直拍反手台内拧拉
b. Backhand over-the-table twist drive with pen-hold grip

图 3-44 反手台内拧拉
Fig.3-44 Backhand over-the-table twist drive

5. 中远台对拉弧圈球

正手动作要点：

（1）动作幅度稍大，引拍时球拍要低于来球，整个动作的用力方向是从右后向左前上方。

5. Middle and back court counter loop

Forehand movement essentials:

(1) It has a little larger range of movement. When swinging the racket back, the racket should be lower than the oncoming ball. The exertion direction of the whole movement is from the right back direction toward the upper-left front direction.

（2）应充分发挥腿、髋、腰、臂和腕的力量，其中，尤应重视身体重心和前臂的作用。

（3）拍形与台面垂直，触球中部。击球时间为下降前期或高点期，以撞击后的摩擦发力为主。（如图3-45）

(2) You should give full play to the strength of the legs, the hip, the waist, the arm and the wrist among which you should especially pay much attention to the role of the center of body weight and the forearm.

(3) You should contact the middle part of the ball with the angle of the racket vertical to the table-board; and hit the ball at its early descending stage or the peak stage, attaching most importance to the friction force after hitting. (As shown in fig.3-45)

图3-45　正手中远台对拉弧圈球

Fig.3-45 Middle and back court counter loop

反手动作要点：

（1）动作幅度稍大，引拍时球拍要低于来球，击球点不宜离身体太近。

（2）充分利用肘关节的杠杆作用，先支肘，再收肘，借以增加前臂的挥摆幅度和力量。

（3）中远台发力拉的击球时间为下降期，但不可过分低于台面。（如图 3-46）

Backhand movement essentials:

(1) It has a little bit larger range of movement. When swinging the racket back, the racket should be lower than the oncoming ball. The hitting point should not be too close to the body.

(2) You should make full use of the lever effect of the elbow joint; and first raise the elbow and then draw it back so as to increase the swing range and force of the forearm.

(3) When looping forcefully from the middle and back court, you should hit the ball at its descending stage, but should not be too much below the table-board. (As shown in fig.3-46)

图 3-46　反手中远台对拉弧圈球

Fig.3-46　Backhand middle and back court counter loop

6. 弧圈球的练习方法

（1）徒手模仿弧圈球击球动作练习。

（2）连续拉发来的下旋球练习。

（3）连续拉削球练习。

（4）连续拧拉发来的台内下旋球练习。

（5）连续拉推挡球练习。

（6）对搓中固定线路拉斜、直线练习。

（7）发球抢拉、抢冲练习。

（8）先拉加转弧圈球，再拉前冲弧圈球练习。

（9）中远台对拉练习。

第八节
防守性技术

1. 削球技术

削球是一种防御性技术，具有稳健性好、冒险性小的特点，它主要通过旋转变化和落点变化控制对方，并伺机反攻得分。

6. Training method for loop drives

(1) Imitate the movements of loop drives with the racket hand on site without the ball, experiencing the movement essentials.

(2) Return backspin serves with loop drives in succession.

(3) Return chops with loop drives in succession.

(4) Return backspin serves within the playing surface with the backhand over-the-table twist drive, in succession.

(5) Return blocks with loop drives in succession.

(6) Loop to the fixed crosscourt lines and straight lines in counter pushes.

(7) Practice looping first after your serve.

(8) Practice doing the heavy-spin loop (also known as high loop) first, and then do the accelerated loop.

(9) Practice countering loops from the middle and back court.

Section 8
Defensive techniques

1. Chop techniques

Chop is a defensive technique featured with good sureness small risk-taking, which is used to control the opponent mainly through the changes of spin and placement awaiting an opportunity to counterattack for scoring.

（1）削一般拉球。

①正手削球。

右脚稍后，身体略向右侧，双膝微屈，拍形竖立，引拍至肩高附近。前臂在上臂的带动下，随身体重心的移动向下、向前、向左挥动，于球下降后期击球中下部，向左前下方切球，手腕向下辅助发力控制好拍形，并有一个摩擦球的动作。（如图3-47）

(1) Chopping the ordinary lifted ball.

① Forehand chop.

Put the right foot a little bit in the back and lean the body slightly to the right side, meanwhile, bend somewhat both the knees, and erect angle of the racket swinging it back to about shoulder height. The forearm which is driven by the upper arm should swing downward, forward and towards the left along with the movement of the center of body weight. Hit the middle-lower part of the ball at its late descending stage, and chop it toward the lower-left front direction. In the meantime, the wrist should put forth its auxiliary strength downwards and control the angle of the racket well; furthermore it should have a friction movement to the ball. (As shown in fig.3-47)

1　　　2　　　3　　　4

a. 横拍正手削球

a.Forehand chop with shake-hand grip

1　　　　　　　2　　　　　　　3　　　　　　　4

b. 直拍正手削球
b.Forehand chop with pen–hold grip

图 3-47　正手削球
Fig.3-47　Forehand shop

②反手削球。

左脚稍后，身体略向左侧，重心在左脚，手臂自然弯曲，球拍向左上方引至肩高，拍柄朝下。击球时手臂向右前下方挥动，拍面稍后仰，触球瞬间前臂和手腕加速削击球的中下部；击球后上体向右转，球拍随势挥至身体右侧，重心移至右脚。（如图 3-48）

② Backhand chop.

Put your left foot slightly in the back and lean the body a little bit to the left side with the center of body weight on the left foot and the arms and hands bent naturally; and swing the racket back toward the upper left direction to the shoulder height with the racket handle downwards. When hitting the ball, you should swing the arm and hand toward the lower-right front direction with the racket face slightly tilted backward. In the instant of contacting the ball, the forearm and wrist should speed up to chop the middle-lower part of it. After hitting the ball, you should rotate the upper part of the body to the right and swing the racket to the right side of the body along with the inertia, shifting the center of body weight onto the right foot. (As shown in fig.3-48)

a. 横拍反手削球
a.Backhand chop with shake-hand grip

b. 直拍反手削球
b.Backhand chop with pen-hold grip

图 3-48　反手削球
Fig.3-48　Backhand shop

（2）削转与不转球。

①正手削加转球。

击球前，向身体的右侧上方引拍，拍形稍后仰，目视来球。击球时，在来球的高点期或下降前期接触球的中下部，向前下方发力摩擦，当接近球底部时，手腕发力摩擦，手腕的发力方向和前臂保持一致，同时要转体转腰以辅

(2) Heavy-spin and no-spin chop.

① Forehand heavy-spin chop.

Before hitting the ball, you should swing the racket back toward the upper right side of the body with the racket face slightly tilted backward, looking at the oncoming ball. When hitting the ball, you should contact the middle-lower part of the oncoming ball at its peak stage or the early descending stage, grazing it forcefully forward and downward. When the racket face is close to the bottom of the ball, the wrist should put forth strength for friction, and the exertion direction of the wrist should be kept

助发力。击球后,迅速还原,准备下一板击球。

②正手削不转球。

击球前,球拍稍立起,拍面接近垂直。击球时,前臂将球用力向前送出而不摩擦球,手腕固定,击球的中部。击球后,迅速还原,准备下一板击球。

③反手削加转球。

击球前,向身体的左侧上方引拍,球拍稍后仰。击球时,前臂外展,向前下方发力摩擦,在接近球的底部时,手腕加力,这时手腕要相对固定。击球后,迅速还原,准备下一板击球。

④反手削不转球。

击球前,右脚稍前,左脚稍后,身体向左侧偏斜,向身体的左后侧上方引拍,球拍稍立起。击球时,在下降前期击球中部,手腕相对固定,前臂手腕将球向前送,在球要离开的时候,前臂再做外展动作,使球拍不对球产生摩

the same with that of the forearm. At the same time, you should rotate your body and waist to give auxiliary force. After hitting the ball, you should quickly recover and get ready for the next stroke.

② Forehand no-spin chop.

Before hitting the ball, you should erect the racket slightly with the racket face close to vertical. When hitting the ball, the forearm should carry the ball forward forcefully with the wrist fixed without friction hitting the middle part of it. After hitting the ball, you should recover quickly and get ready for the next stroke.

③ Backhand heavy-spin chop.

Before hitting the ball, you should swing the racket back toward the upper left side of the body with the racket face slightly tilted backward. When hitting the ball, you should extend the forearm outwards to graze it forwards and downwards forcefully. When the racket face is close to the bottom of the ball, the wrist should give strength, and at this time, the wrist should be relatively fixed.After hitting the ball, you should recover quickly and get ready for the next stroke.

④ Backhand no-spin chop.

Before hitting the ball, put the right foot somewhat in the front and the left foot slightly in the back with the body leaned to the left side. you should swing the racket back toward the upper left back direction with the racket face slightly erected. When hitting the ball, you should hit the middle part of it at its early descending stage with the wrist relatively fixed. The forearm and wrist should carry the ball forward, and the forearm should not do the movement of extending until the ball is leaving the racket face, which makes the

擦，也就是削出相对不转的球。击球后，迅速还原，准备下一板击球。

（3）削不同性能的来球。

①削突击球。

突击球速度快、力量大，削球时脚步移动要快，一般用单步、跳步或跨步迅速后移，手臂向上快速引拍，拍面稍垂直，于球下降前期切击球中下部，击球瞬间手腕相对固定，由上向下用力压球，借以抵消来球的向上反弹力。（如图3-49）

racket not produce friction to the ball, so as to chop the no-spin ball. After hitting the ball, you should recover quickly and get ready for the next stroke.

(3) Chopping the oncoming ball of different properties.

① Chopping a sudden attacking ball.

The sudden attacking ball has fast speed and great force, when chopping it your footwork should be fast. Generally, you should move back quickly with the single step, hop step or stride step; and the arm and hand should swing the racket upwards rapidly with the racket face slightly vertical to hit the middle-lower part of the ball at its early descending stage. At the instant of hitting the ball, the wrist should be relatively fixed; and you should press the ball forcefully from top to bottom so as to counteract the upward bounciness of the oncoming ball. (As shown in fig.3-49)

1　　　　　2　　　　　3　　　　　4

a. 横拍正手近台削接突击球

a. Chopping a sudden attacking ball by forehand with shake-hand grip in the close-table position

b. 横拍反手远台前送削接突击球

b.Forward chopping a sudden attacking ball by backhand with shake-hand grip in the close-table position

c. 横拍反手远台前送削接突击球

c.Forward chopping a sudden attacking ball by backhand with shake-hand grip from the back court

d. 直拍正手远台前送削接突击球

d.Forward chopping a sudden attacking ball by forehand with pen-hold grip from the back court

图 3-49 削接突击球

Fig.3-49 Chopping a sudden attacking ball

②削追身球。

对方攻球至中路追身，因受身体妨碍，影响手臂的活动，削球比较困难，需根据实际情况迅速移动，选用正手或反手削球。用正手削追身球时，右脚后撤，腰向右转，收腹。引拍时上臂靠近身体，前臂向右上方提起，拍面竖直，于下降前期击球中下部。触球瞬间，前臂和手腕向前下方用力压球下切，重心移至左脚。（如图3-50）

② Chopping a body hit.

It is more difficult to chop the body hit to the middle route attacked by your opponent due to the fact that the movement of the arm is affected by the obstruction of the body. you should move promptly to select and use the forehand chopping or the backhand chopping according to the actual situation. When using the forehand to chop the body hit, you should step the right foot back and rotate the waist to the right with the abdomen drawn in. When swinging the racket back, you should make the upper arm near the body and lift the forearm to the upper right with the racket face upright; and hit the middle-lower part of the ball at its early descending stage. At the instant of contacting the ball, you should use the forearm and wrist to hold down and chop the ball forwards and downwards forcefully, shifting the center of body weight onto the left foot. (As shown in fig.3-50)

图 3-50 横拍让位正手削追身球

Fig.3-50 Chopping a body hit by the forehand with shake-hand grip through giving the way

反手削追身球时，左脚后撤，腰向左转，收腹。引拍时，上臂紧贴身体，前臂将球拍引至胸前，拍面竖直，于下降前期击球中下部。触球瞬间，前臂向右前下方下切，压低弧线。（如图 3-51）

When using the backhand to chop the body hit, you should step the left foot back and rotate the waist to the left with the abdomen drawn in. When swinging the racket back, you should make the upper arm cling to the body and swing the racket to the front of your chest by the forearm with the racket face upright; and hit the middle-lower part of the ball at its early descending stage. At the instant of contacting the ball, you should use the forearm to chop down the ball toward the lower-right front direction pressing the trajectory lower. (As shown in fig.3-51)

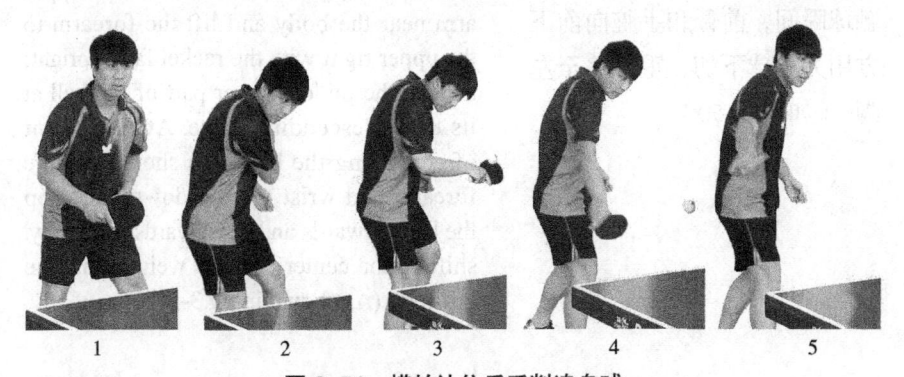

1　　　2　　　3　　　4　　　5

图 3-51　横拍让位反手削追身球

Fig.3-51　Chopping a body hit by the backhand with shake-hand grip through giving the way

当来球迅速、直冲中路、来不及移步让位时，可迅速直身收腹、含胸、提踵，同时球拍上举，再向前下方用力将球削出。（如图 3-52）

When the oncoming ball is rushing straight to the middle route quickly and it's too late for you to move your steps to give the way, you can straighten the body quickly, draw the abdomen in, make the chest inward and raise your heels. And in the meantime, you should lift up the racket and then chop out the ball forwards and downwards forcefully. (As shown in fig.3-52)

图 3-52 横拍收腹含胸削追身球

Fig.3-52 Chopping a body hit with shake-hand grip by making the abdomen drawn in and the chest inward

（4）削弧圈球。

①削加转弧圈球。

加转弧圈球上旋力强，触拍后反弹力很大，削球容易回出高球或出界，因此，削加转弧圈球时击球时间要晚，击球点要低，动作幅度要大。正手削球时左脚在前，两脚的间距稍大，重心在右脚，向后引拍幅度加大，拍面竖直，于球下降前期或后期向下切击球的中部，击球瞬间有一个先下压、后摩擦、再推送的动作，手腕切忌晃动。削弧圈球时应特别注意判断，尽早移

(4) Chopping loop drives.

① Chopping the heavy-spin loop.

The heavy-spin loop has a strong topspin force, after contacting the racket it will bounce greatly, which will cause your chopping to make a high ball or out of bounds. Therefore, when chopping the heavy-spin loop the time of hitting the ball should be late, the hitting point should be lower and the movement range should be large. When chopping with the forehand, you should put the left foot in the front with a slightly larger space between your two feet and the center of body weight on the right foot. You should increase the range of swinging the racket backward with the racket face upright and chop downwards to hit the middle part of the ball at its early descending or late descending stage. At the instant of hitting the ball, you should do a movement composed of the steps which are pressing down first, then grazing and next pushing; here you must guard against shaking the wrist. When chopping the heavy-spin loop, you should pay

动选位，争取在最佳击球位置（一般在右腹前）击球。（如图 3-53）

special attention to judgment so as to move to select position as soon as possible, trying hard to hit the ball in the optimal position (generally, in front of the right abdomen). (As shown in fig.3-53)

图 3-53　横拍正手削加转弧圈球
Fig.3-53　Chopping the heavy-spin loop by the forehand with shake-hand grip

反手削加转弧圈球时右脚在前，左脚稍后。击球前，向身体的左后上方引拍，拍形稍后仰，接近垂直，身体向左偏斜，双腿弯曲。

击球时，在来球的下降后期击球的中下部，前臂从上向前下方用力，触球时手腕相对固定，拍形不要过于后仰，弯腰屈膝辅助压低弧线，重心从左脚移至右脚。击球后，迅速还原，准备接下一板来球。（如图 3-54）

When chopping the heavy-spin loop with the backhand, you should put the right foot in the front and the left foot slightly in the back. Before hitting the ball, you should swing the racket back toward the upper-left back direction of your body with the racket face slightly tilted backward approximately vertical; meanwhile, lean the body to the left and bend both legs.

When hitting the ball, you should hit the middle-lower part of the oncoming ball at its late descending stage; and the forearm should put forth its strength from up to the lower front. When contacting the ball, the wrist should be relatively fixed; and the racket face should not be tilted backward too much. You should stoop down and bend your knees assisting to lower the trajectory, and shift the center of body weight from the left foot onto the right foot. After hitting the ball, you should quickly recover and get ready for the next oncoming ball. (As shown in fig.3-54)

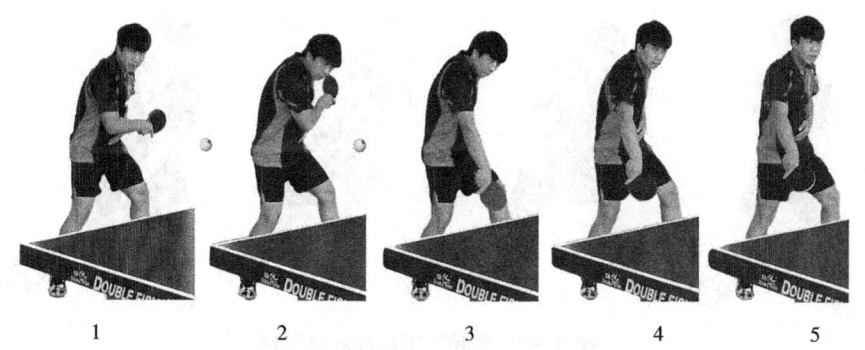

图 3-54 横拍反手削加转弧圈球
Fig.3-54 Chopping the heavy-spin loop by the backhand with shake-hand grip

②削前冲弧圈球。

前冲弧圈球既快又转，削接时要反应快、步法快、动作快，拍形要竖直向下切削，在削接时注意球拍稍向前送，以防下网。

正手削前冲弧圈球：击球前，右脚速向后让位（用单步），身体向右偏斜，手臂迅速上举，拍形接近垂直。击球时，在来球的下降后期击球的中下部，击球时迎着来球手臂连同转腰从上向下压球，重心由右脚移至左脚，触球时手腕相对固定。击球后，迅速还原，准备下一板击球。（如图 3-55）

② Chopping the accelerated loop.

The accelerated loop is fast as well as rotatory; when returning it with chopping you should respond quickly and be fast in footwork and action. And you should chop downwards with the racket face upright and pay attention that you should carry the racket slightly forward when return the ball with chopping in case hit it into the net.

Chopping the accelerated loop with the forehand: before hitting the ball, you should step the right foot backwards rapidly to give the way (with the single step) and lean the body to the right, in the meantime, you should uplift the arm rapidly with the racket face approximately vertical. When hitting the ball, you should hit the middle-lower part of the oncoming ball at its late descending stage. Facing the oncoming ball, you should use the arm and hand to press it from above downward together with the rotation of the waist at the same time, shift the center of body weight from the right foot onto the left foot. When contacting the ball, the wrist should be relatively fixed. After hitting the ball, you should quickly recover and get ready for the next stroke. (As shown in fig.3-55)

图 3-55　横拍正手削前冲弧圈球

Fig.3-55　Chopping the accelerated loop by forehand with shake-hand grip

反手削前冲弧圈球：击球前，左脚迅速向后让位，手臂上举，拍形接近垂直，身体向左偏斜，双腿弯曲。击球时，在来球的下降后期击球的中下部，前臂向前下方用力，触球时手腕相对固定，控制板形同时弯腰曲膝，以辅助压低弧线。击球后，迅速还原，准备下一板击球。（如图 3-56）

Chopping the accelerated loop by the backhand: before hitting the ball, you should move the left foot backward rapidly to give the way and uplift the arm quickly with the racket face close to the vertical at the same time, lean the body to the left and bend both legs. When hitting the ball, you should hit the middle-lower part of the oncoming ball at its late descending stage with the forearm putting forth its strength forwards and downwards. When contacting the ball, you should make the wrist relatively fixed to control the racket angle meanwhile, stoop down your waist and bend knees assisting to lower the trajectory. After hitting the ball, you should quickly recover and get ready for the next stroke. (As shown in fig.3-56)

图 3-56　横拍反手削前冲弧圈球

Fig.3-56　Chopping the accelerated loop by the backhand with shake-hand grip

（5）削球的练习方法。

①徒手模仿削球练习。

②用正反手削对方的发球练习。

③用正反手削斜线、直线球练习。

④削送机会球，由对方扣杀后削突击球或追身球练习。

⑤削转与不转球练习。

⑥削中反攻练习。

2. 放高球技术

放高球是一种防守技术，特点是弧线高，落点远，上旋力强。在被动防御时使用，能消耗对方体力，为调整战术赢得时间，也能增大对方的接球难度或使之失误，起到以守为攻的作用。

正手放高球，击球前，左脚稍前，身体离球台约1米远，腰、髋向右转动，右肩下沉，将球拍引至身体的右侧后下方，拍稍后仰。击球时，上臂由后下方向前上方挥动，前臂和手腕用力向上转动，在来

(5) Training method for chop.

① Practice imitating the movements of chop with the racket hand on site without the ball.

② Returning serves from the opponent with the forehand chop and backhand chop.

③ Returning a ball in the crosscourt lines and the straight lines with the forehand chop and backhand chop.

④ First chop to make a chance ball for the opponent, and then practice chopping a sudden attacking ball or a body hit after the smash of the opponent.

⑤ Practice the heavy-spin and no-spin chop.

⑥ Practice launching a counteroffensive amid chops.

2. Techniques of high lobbing

Lobbing is a kind of defensive technique, which has the characteristics of high trajectory, distant placement and strong force of topspin. Used in passive defense it can take away the physical strength of an opponent to gain time for modulating your tactics and can also increase the difficulty for the opponent to return the ball or make the opponent misplay, playing the role of taking defense as offense.

Forehand lobbing: before hitting the ball, put the left foot slightly in the front with the body about 1 m away from the table, and rotate the waist and hip to the right lowering down the right shoulder; and swing the racket back to the lower position of the right back side of the body with the racket tilted backwards. When hitting the ball, you should swing the upper arm from the lower back toward the upper front with the forearm and wrist putting forth strength to turn upward, and graze

球的下降期摩擦球的中部或中部偏下位置。以整个手臂的发力为主，身体重心从右脚移至左脚。击球后，迅速调整重心并立即还原。（如图 3-57）

the middle part or the middle lower part of the oncoming ball at its descending stage. You should give first place to the strength put forth by the entire arm and hand; and shift the center of body weight from the right foot onto the left foot. After hitting the ball, you should quickly adjust the center of body weight and recover immediately. (As shown in fig.3-57a)

图 3-57 横拍正手放高球
Fig.3-57 Forehand lobbing with shake-hand grip

反手放高球，击球前，右脚稍前，站位离球台约1米远，前臂下沉，将球拍引至身体左后下方。击球时，上臂向前上方挥动，前臂随之向上拉起，拍面稍前倾，在来球跳至下降后期摩擦球的中上部。击球后，以整个手臂发力为主，身体重心从左脚移至右脚。（如图3-58）

Backhand lobbing: before hitting the ball, put the right foot slightly in the front with your position more than 1 m away from the table, and swing the racket back to the lower position of the left back side of the body. When hitting the ball, you should swing the upper arm forwards and upwards and lift the forearm up accordingly with the racket face tilted a little bit forward. When the oncoming ball bounces to its late descending stage you should graze the middle-upper part of it. After hitting the ball, you should give first place to the strength put forth by the entire arm and hand, shifting the center of body weight from the left foot onto the right foot.(As shown in fig.3-58)

图 3-58 横拍反手放高球
Fig.3-58 Backhand lobbing with shake-hand grip

第四章
乒乓球的基本战术与运用

Chapter 4
Basic tactics of table tennis and the application

第一节
乒乓球基本战术

乒乓球的基本战术是指运动员根据自己和对方实力的对比，积极发挥自己的长处，合理地运用技术，达到获胜的目的。

1. 发球抢攻战术

发球抢攻是乒乓球运动员的重要战术之一。近年来，世界各种类型打法的运动员都越来越重视这一战术，并使之有了很大发展。具体方法有：

（1）正手发转与不转球结合落点变化进行抢攻。

①发相同落点的转与不转下旋球（近网）。一般以发至中路或对方正手小三角短球为主，先发转后发不转或先发不转再发转球，然后进行抢攻。（如图4-1）

Section 1
Basic tactics of table tennis

The basic tactics of table tennis mean that a player should actively bring his (her) own strengths into play and reasonably apply the techniques to achieve the purpose of winning on the basis of the comparison of actual power between himself (herself) and the opponent.

1. The tactic of attacking after service

Attacking after service is one of the important tactics for table tennis players. In recent years, players with all kinds of style over the world have paid more and more attention to the tactic, and make it have a very big development. Specific methods are as follows:

(1) Carrying out a preemptive attack after the forehand spin and no-spin serves in combination with the placement change.

① You can make backspin serves with spin and no-spin to the same placement (net zone). Generally, give priority to the middle route serve or the short serve to the forehand small triangle of the opponent. You can first do a spin serve and then make a no-spin serve or serve in reverse; afterwards, carry out a preemptive attack. (As shown in fig.4-1)

图 4-1　发相同落点的转与不转下旋球

Fig.4-1　Backspin serves of spin and no-spin to the same placement

②发不同落点的转与不转下旋球。发短球后，突然发长球进行抢攻。（如图 4-2）

② You can make backspin serves with spin and no-spin to different placements. After the short serve you can suddenly deliver a long serve to launch a preemptive attack. (As shown in fig.4-2)

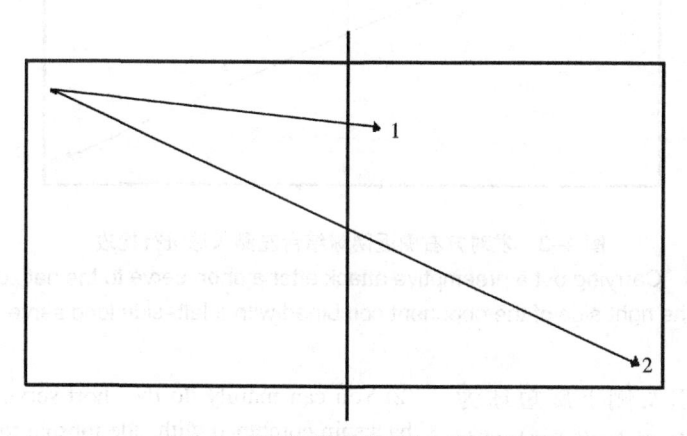

图 4-2　发不同落点的转与不转下旋球

Fig.4-2　Backspin serves of spin and no-spin to different placements

（2）侧身正手发高低抛左侧上，下旋球后进行抢攻。

①以发侧下旋短球为主，结合侧上旋至对方右侧近网处，使对方难以抢攻，从而为自己抢拉（攻）创造机会。在此基础上，突然发出角度大的长球（以急下旋为主）至对方左侧台区，使对方难以发力，难以拉攻，为自己侧身或正手抢攻创造机会。（如图 4-3）

(2) Carrying out a preemptive attack after the sideways high or low toss serve of the left-side topspin or left-side backspin with forehand.

① You can mainly make the short serve of side backspin combined with side topspin to the net zone on the right side of the opponent, which will make the opponent hard to launch an attack; thereby create opportunities for yourself to loop (attack) first. And on this basis you can make a long serve (mainly the fast backspin) of large angle suddenly to the left-side playing surface of the opponent, which will make the opponent hard to put forth strength and do a topspin drive; thereby create opportunities for yourself to step sideways or attack with the forehand. (As shown in fig.4-3)

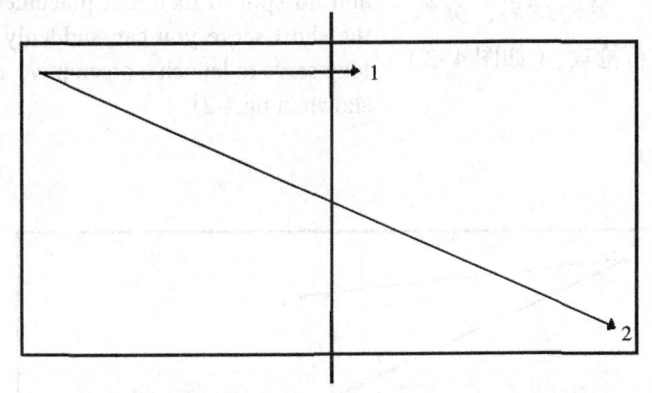

图 4-3　发对方右侧近网球结合左侧长球进行抢攻

Fig.4-3　Carrying out a preemptive attack after a short serve to the net zone on the right side of the opponent combined with a left-side long serve

②以发侧下旋短球为主，结合侧上旋至对方左侧近网处，使对方难以上手，然后抢攻。在此基础上，突然发出对方正手直线长球，出其不意，然后侧身或正手抢攻。（如图 4-4）

② You can mainly do the short serve of side backspin combined with side topspin to the net zone on the left side of the opponent, which will make the opponent hard to get ready for an attack, and then you can instead find opportunities to attack. And based on it you can make a long serve of straight line suddenly to the forehand of the opponent at unawares, then step sideways or attack with the forehand. (As shown in fig.4-4)

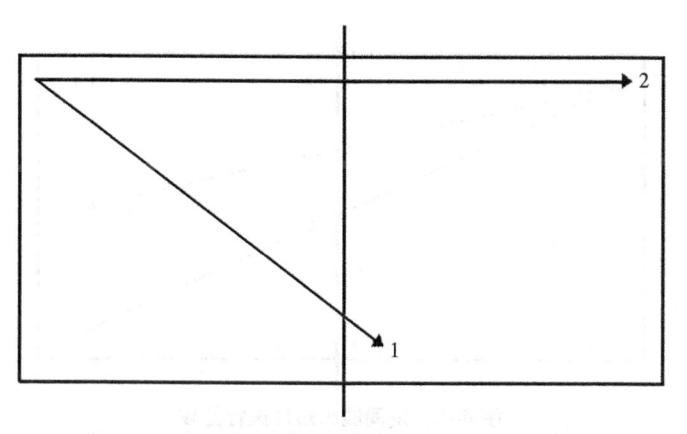

图 4-4　发对方左侧近网球结合右侧长球进行抢攻

Fig.4-4　Carrying out a preemptive attack after a short serve to the net zone on the left side of the opponent combined with a right-side long serve

③以发同线长短球为主抢攻。这种发球抢攻战术主要用来对付横拍削球手。其中比较有效的是发中长、中短侧上（下）旋球。

因为横拍削球手接中路近网短球和中路追身长球时较难变化旋转，其回球质量会下降，陷入被动。同时，对付横拍两面攻和两面拉的选手也可采用这种战术。也能获得较好效果。（如图4-5）

③ You can primarily make the long and short serves to the same line for launching a preemptive attack. This tactic of attacking after service is mainly used to cope with the choppers with shake-hand grip, of which the more effective way is to make the long and short serves of side topspin (side backspin) to the middle route.

Since it is more difficult for the choppers of shake-hand grip to change the spin of the ball when returning a drop shot near the net and a long body hit in the middle route. So, the quality of their returns will be reduced and they will be caught in passiveness. And at the same time, this tactic can also be used to cope with the two-winged attackers and the two-winged loopers with shake-hand grip, which can also obtain a good effect. (As shown in fig.4-5)

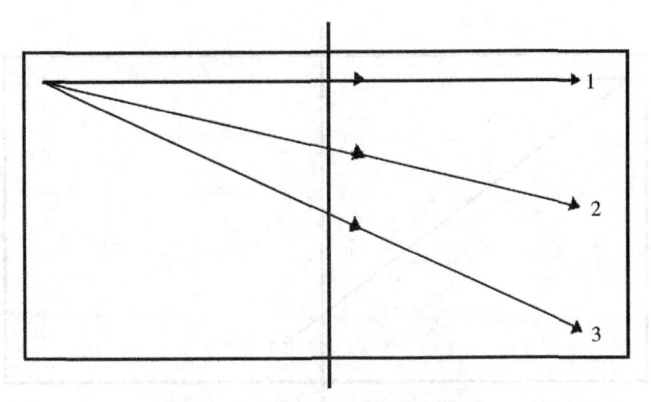

图 4-5　发同线长短球进行抢攻

Fig.4-5　Launching a preemptive attack after the long and short serves to the same line

（3）发急球与侧上、下旋转球相结合，进行抢攻。

①急球与上、下旋球相结合。反手发急上旋球至对方反手后，侧身抢攻，要求急球要发得急、快、力量大、线路长。擅长反手推挡的选手或遇到对方反手推攻较差的选手，可发急下旋后用推挡紧压对方反手再伺机侧身攻。为增加上述战术的效果，最好与发左（右）方短侧上（下）旋球配合运用，以长短牵制对方。（如图 4-6）

(3) Carrying out a preemptive attack after the drive serve combined with the side topspin and the side backspin serves.

①Combining the drive serve with the topspin and backspin serves. You can launch a sideways attack after a backhand serve of fast heavy topspin to the backhand location of the opponent demanding that the drive serve should be snap, fast, powerful and long. If you are good at backhand block or cope with an opponent whose backhand block and attack techniques are poorer, you can first make a serve of fast heavy backspin and press to the backhand of the opponent with block, and then await an opportunity to launch a sideways attack. In order to increase the effect of above-mentioned tactics you should better cooperatively use short serves of side topspin (side backspin) to the left (the right) side of the opponent containing him (or her) with the long and short serves. (As shown in fig.4-6)

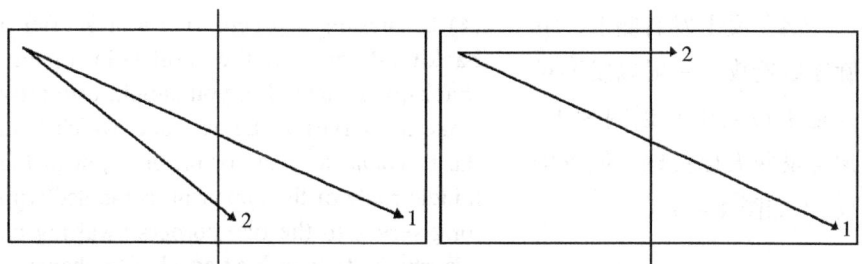

图 4-6　发急球与左（右）方短侧上（下）旋球配合运用
Fig.4-6　Combining the drive serve with the short serves of side topspin (side backspin) to the left (the right) side

②侧上、下旋球与急球结合发至不同落点。发侧上或侧下旋球与急球结合至不同落点，以发侧上或侧下为主配合发右角急球，发正手右大角急球配合左大角急球，伺机抢攻。（如图 4-7）

② Making the topspin or backspin serves and the drive serves to different placements in combination: you can make serves of the side topspin or side backspin combined with the drive serve to different placements. You should primarily make serves of the side topspin or side backspin cooperating with the drive serve to the right corner. You can also make a forehand drive serve to the right corner combined with a drive serve to the left corner awaiting an opportunity to launch an attack. (As shown in fig.4-7)

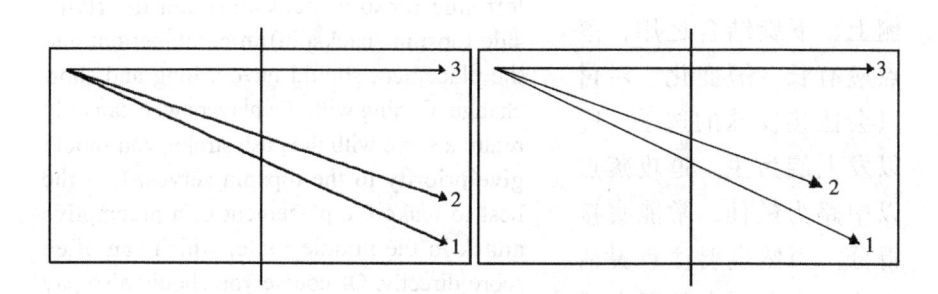

图 4-7　侧上、下旋球与急球结合发至不同落点
Fig.4-7　Making serves of the side topspin or side backspin combined with the drive serve to different placements

（4）反手发右侧上、下旋球后抢攻。一般以发至对方正手位或中右近网为主，配合发两大角长球，伺机抢攻。(如图4-8)

(4) Launching a preemptive attack after a backhand serve of the right-side topspin (backspin). Generally, you should primarily make the serves to the net zone, which is in the forehand location or on the right of the middle route of the opponent, combined with long serves to the two corners awaiting an opportunity to launch an attack. (As shown in fig.4-8)

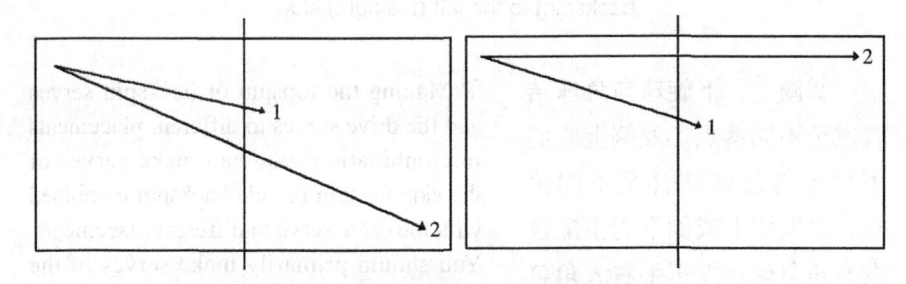

图 4-8　反手发右侧上、下旋球后抢攻

Fig.4-8　Launching a preemptive attack after a backhand serve of the right-side topspin or the right-side backspin

（5）下蹲发球后抢攻。可以将左侧上、下旋与右侧上、下旋结合运用，落点应有长、短变化，对付只会搓接发球的选手，应以发上旋为主。抢攻落点以中路为最佳，常能直接得分。当然也要注意灵活变化，攻击对方的弱点或声东击西。(如图4-9)

(5) Launching a preemptive attack after a squatting serve. You can use serves of the left-side topspin (backspin) and the right-side topspin (backspin) in combination; and the placement should have a long and short change. Coping with the players who can only return a serve with the push stroke, you should give priority to the topspin serves. It is the best to make the placement of a preemptive attack in the middle route, which can often score directly. Of course you should also pay attention to the nimble change, and attack the opponent's weaknesses or sell the dummy. (As shown in fig.4-9)

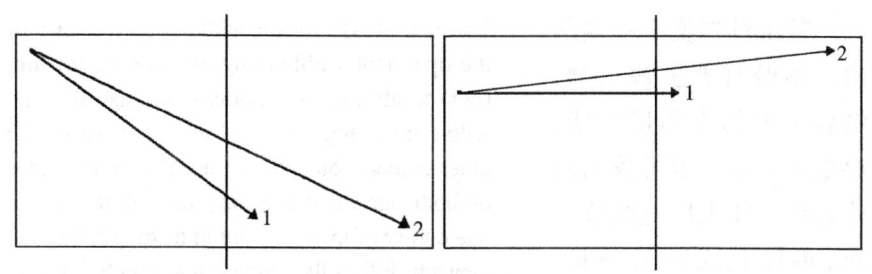

图 4-9 攻击对方的弱点或声东击西
Fig.4-9 Attacking the weaknesses of an opponent or selling the dummy

2. 对攻战术

对攻，是进攻类打法在相互对抗时，双方利用速度、旋转、落点变化和力量轻重来控制对方，力争主动的一种重要手段。对攻战术主要依靠左推右攻或正、反手攻结合的打法，它具有快速多变的特点，达到调动、攻击对方的目的。具体方法有：

（1）攻两角战术。

①对角攻击和双边直线。（如图 4-10）

2. The tactic of counter drive

When the players of attacking play competing against each other, counter drive is an important means by which both sides use the change of speed, spin and placement together with heavy and light force to control the opponent, and strive to gain the initiative. The tactic of counter drive relies mainly on backhand block with forehand attack or the combinative two-winged attack play, which has the rapid and changeable charactcristics thus achieving the goal of moving and attacking the opponent. The specific methods are as follows:

(1) The tactic of attacking the two corners.

① Attacking in crosscourt lines and straight lines on both sides .(As shown in fig.4-10)

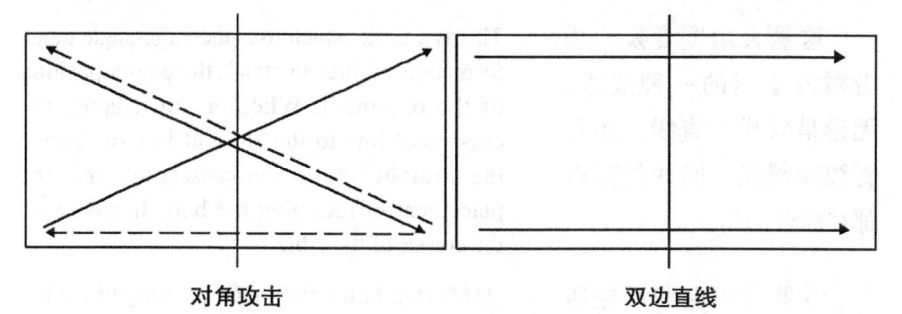

对角攻击
Attacking in crosscourt lines

双边直线
Attacking in straight lines on both sides

图 4-10 对角攻击和双边直线
Fig.4-10 Attacking in crosscourt lines and straight lines on both sides

紧压对方反手一侧的角，不给对方进攻机会，结合突然的大角度变线，再攻另一角。也可采用双边直线，即先以直线攻一角，再以直线攻另一角。此战术是靠攻击对方左右两个大角，使其顾此失彼，从而占据主动。一般用于应对步法缓慢、动作较慢的对手。

②逢斜变直、逢直变斜。（如图4-11）

You can press to the backhand-side corner of the opponent withholding any chance for him (her) to attack, and suddenly change the line with a large angle in combination to attack the other corner. You can also use the straight lines on both sides, that is to say, you can first attack one corner of the opponent in a straight line and then attack the other corner in a straight line too. Depend on attacking the left and right corners of the opponent, this tactic can make him (her) attend to one thing and lose another so as to gain the initiative for you. Thus the tactic is commonly used to cope with the players whose footwork and movement are slower.

② Changing the crosscourt line to the straight line and changing the straight line to the crosscourt line. (As shown in fig.4-11)

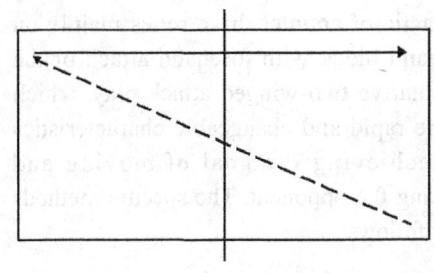

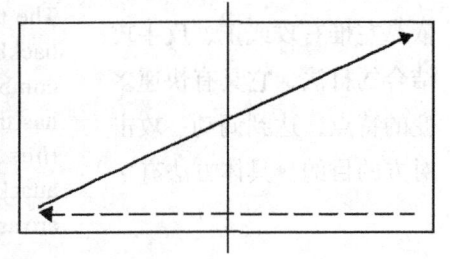

图4-11　逢斜变直、逢直变斜

Fig.4-11　Changing the crosscourt line to the straight line and changing the straight line to the crosscourt line

这是大角度变换、袭击对方空当的一种战术。无论是斜线变直线，还是直线变斜线，回球的落点都在球台的角上。

③调右压左和调左压右。这两种战术的采用要根据对手的实际情况来决

This is a tactic which uses the large-angle transformation of lines to attack the empty position of the opponent. Whether you change the crosscourt line to the straight line or change the straight line to the crosscourt line, the placement of returning the ball should be on the corner of the table.

③ Moving to the right then pressing to the left and moving to the left then pressing to the right. The adoption of these two tactics should be determined according to the opponent's

定。所谓调右压左就是先打对方正手，将其调动到正手位并迫其离台后再打其反手位。这种战术适用于右手执拍且擅长侧身进攻的选手，或用来应对正手位进攻能力不很强、反手位只能近台、不擅长离台的直拍快攻手。运用此战术应注意：调正手的这板球要凶，压反手的球角度要大。（如图 4-12）

actual situation. What is called moving to the right then pressing to the left, precisely means that first you hit the ball to the opponent's forehand position moving him to the forehand location and forcing him away from the table; and then attack his backhand location. This tactic is applicable to the players who hold the racket with the right hand and are good at sideways attack, or used to cope with the players of pen-hold fast attack whose forehand attacking ability is not very strong meanwhile, the backhand is not very good at playing in the middle and back court and can only play at short court. When using this tactic, you should pay attention: the stroke which will move the opponent to the forehand position should be fierce; and the stroke pressing to the backhand location of the opponent should be played with a large angle. (As shown in fig.4-12)

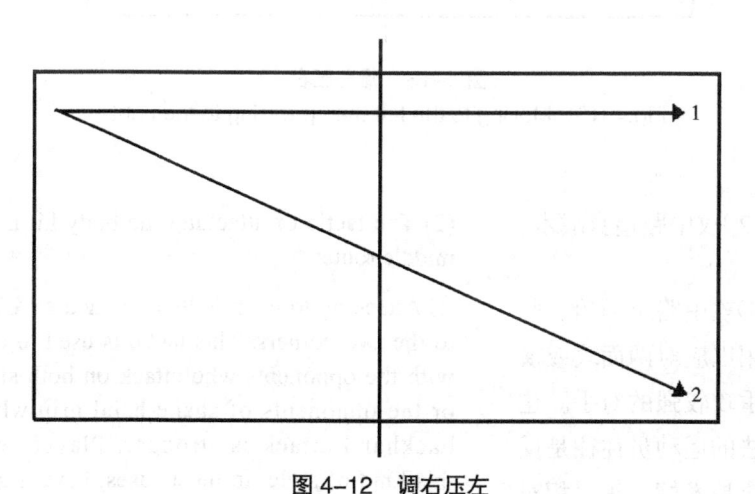

图 4-12　调右压左

Fig.4-12　Moving to the right then pressing to the left

所谓调左压右就是先打对方反手，将其压制在反手位，然后再打其正手位。这种战术适用于应对正手位攻击力不强的选手。（如图4-13）

What is called moving to the left then pressing to the right, precisely means that first you hit the ball to the opponent's backhand position holding down him to the backhand location; and then attack his forehand location. This tactic is suitable for coping with the players whose forehand attacking ability is not very strong. (As shown in fig.4-13)

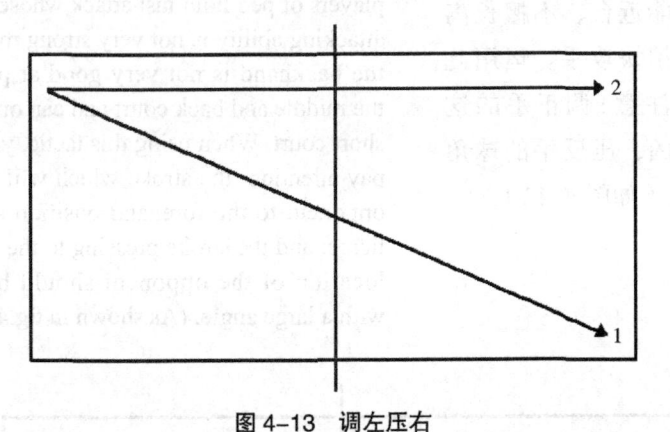

图 4-13 调左压右
Fig.4-13 Moving to the left then pressing to the right

（2）攻中路追身战术。

① 攻中路杀两角。此战术用以应对两面攻或横拍反手攻较强的对手。这类打法的运动员往往是反手进攻技术好、正手相对较弱，中路更是其弱中之弱。可先用推挡或反手攻压住对方的中路或正手，伺机杀反手。（如图4-14）

(2) The tactic of attacking the body hit in the middle route.

① Attacking to the middle route and smashing to the two corners. This tactic is used to cope with the opponents who attack on both sides, or the opponents of shake-hand grip whose backhand attack is stronger. Players with this kind of style, in most cases, have a good backhand attack technique and the forehand is relatively weak; the middle route is the weakest of their weaknesses. You can first use the block or backhand attack to hold down the middle route or the forehand location of the opponent awaiting an opportunity to hit to the backhand position. (As shown in fig.4-14)

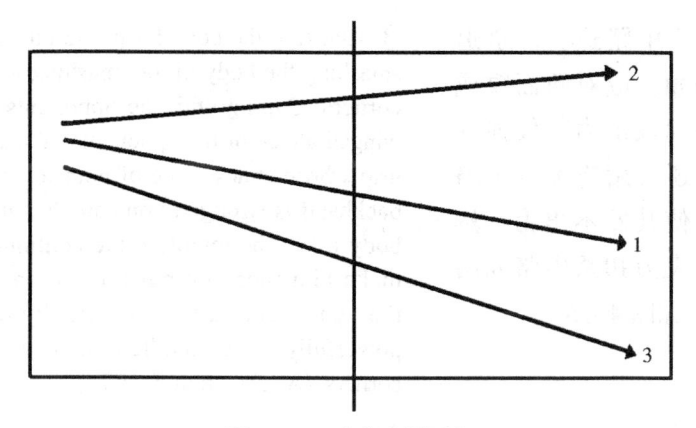

图 4-14 攻中路杀两角

Fig.4-14 Attacking to the middle route and smashing to the two corners

②攻两角杀中路。此战术用以应对对方两面攻或横拍左右两面都不怎么凶狠的选手，而自己是反手相持能力较强，正手攻击力较凶狠的选手。（如图 4-15）

② Attacking to the two corners and hitting to the middle route: This tactic is used to cope with the opponents of two-winged attack or the opponents of shake-hand grip whose backhand and forehand attacks are both not very fierce. Instead you, yourself are the player who has a stronger backhand ability in stalemate and fierce forehand attack. (As shown in fig.4-15)

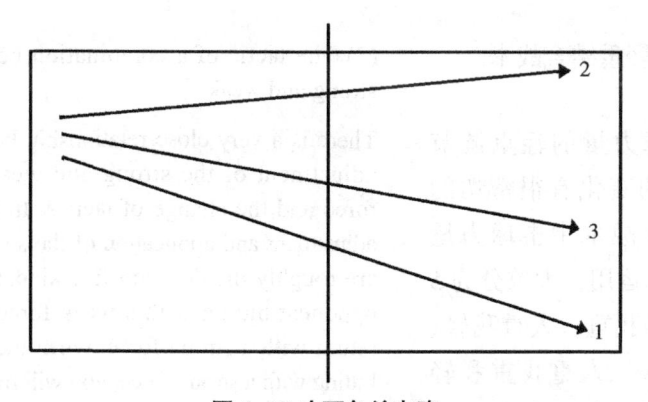

图 4-15 攻两角杀中路

Fig.4-15 Attacking to the two corners and smashing to the middle route

③攻中路追身，杀追身或两角。应对两面攻或横拍两面攻击力都较强的对手，还可用连续攻中路追身，使其发不出力，然后伺机发力扣杀中路或两大角。（如图4-16）

③Attacking the body hit in the middle route, smashing the body hit or smashing to the two corners. Coping with the opponents of two-winged attack or the opponents of shake-hand grip whose attack force of both forehand and backhand is stronger, you can also attack the body hit in the middle route continuously to make him (her) not put forth strength. And then you can await an opportunity to smash powerfully to the middle route or to the two corners. (As shown in fig.4-16)

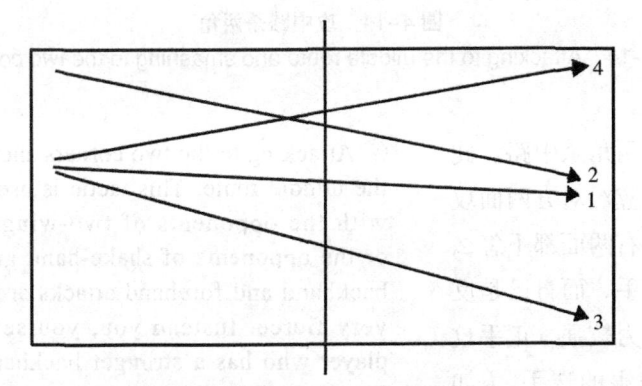

图4-16 攻中路追身，杀追身或两角

Fig.4-16 Attacking the body hit in the middle route, smashing the body hit or smashing to the two corners

（3）轻重结合战术。

击球力量的轻重调节与战术的变化有很密切的关系。在战术中击球力量的调节和运用，大致分为5种：人轻我重、人重我轻、人轻我轻、人重我重和轻重结合。比如，在应对站位中台的两面拉（攻）选手，一般先用加力推（攻）将

(3) The tactic of a combination between the strong and weak.

There is a very close relationship between the adjustment of the strong and weak striking force and the change of tactics. In tactics the adjustment and application of the striking force are roughly divided into five kinds: when the opponent hitting with a weak force, you will return with a strong force; when the opponent hitting with a strong force, you will return with a weak force; and when the opponent hitting with a weak force, you will return with a weak force too; when the opponent hitting with a strong force, you will return with a strong force too; and

对方压下去，再用减力挡将其诱上来，然后伺机大力扣杀。具体方法有：

①同线路轻重球结合运用。

②不同线路轻重球结合运用。先以轻拉或挡球引对方靠前回接，再以突击或加力推攻击对方的相反方向。

③中路轻重球结合，先以中路近网球引对方上前回球，再突击对方中路追身长球。

3. 拉攻战术

拉攻是进攻型打法应对削球打法的主要战术，主要通过拉球落点、旋转和力量的变化制造机会，伺机突击、抢冲和扣杀。具体方法有：

（1）拉左杀右或拉右杀左战术。此战术实际上是拉对方一边杀另一边。一般先拉到对方削球旋转变化不强

you hit the ball with a strong or weak force in combination. For example, when coping with a player of two-winged loop (attack) who stands at the middle court, generally, you should first press him down with the accentuated block (attack), and next seduce him to come up with the stop-block shot; and then await an opportunity to smash powerfully. The specific methods are as follows:

① You can hit the ball to the same line with a strong or weak force in combination.

② You can hit the ball to different lines with a strong or weak force in combination. First, with light loops or the block you can seduce the opponent to come up to return and then make a sudden attack or accentuated block toward the opposite side of the opponent.

③ You can hit the ball to the middle route with a strong or weak force in combination. First, with the drop shot in the middle route you can seduce the opponent to come up to return and then make a sudden attack of deep body-hit in the middle route of the opponent.

3. The tactic of topspin drive

The tactic of topspin drive is the main tactic for the players of attacking play to cope with the players of chopping play, by which you can primarily creates an opportunity through the change of placement, spin and force of the topspin drive awaiting an opportunity to assault with the sound loop and powerful smash. The specific methods are as follows:

(1) You can lift drive to the left and smash to the right or lift drive to the right and smash to the left. This tactic actually means that you lift drive to one side of the opponent and smash to the other side. Generally, you should first lift drive to the side on which the opponent cannot

或攻势较弱的一边，出现机会后杀另一边，双边直线或对角攻击。

（2）拉中路杀两角或拉两角杀中路战术。拉中路杀两角，是从中路寻找机会，然后杀两角得分。一般用于应对以逼角为主或落点控制较好的选手。先拉中路，迫使对方忙于让位，难以逼角或控制落点，这样就能获得较多的扣杀、抢冲的机会。拉两角杀中路，是先从两角找机会，然后突击中路得分。中路追身球是削球选手的共同弱点，特别是对正反手顶重板比较稳的削球手，中路是其最好的突破口。

（3）拉直杀斜或拉斜杀直战术。这两个战术相比较而言，拉斜杀直时拉球比较保险、稳健，杀直线虽威胁大，但技术难度也较大；拉直杀斜时拉球难度稍大，但杀斜线的难度降低，命中率高。因此，这两个战术的使用需根据

make changes of spin strongly when chopping or he can do a weaker offensive. After a chance appears you should smash to the other side in straight lines on both sides or smash crosscourt.

(2) You can lift drive to the middle route and smash to the two corners or lift drive to the two corners and smash to the middle route. Lift driving to the middle route and smashing to the two corners mean that you should look for opportunities from the middle route and then smash to the two corners to score. And the tactic is commonly used to cope with the players who primarily press in corners or have a better control of placement. So, you should lift drive to the middle route making the opponent busy with giving way and hard to press in corners or control the placement. In this way you can get more opportunities to smash and loop first. Lift driving to the two corners and smashing to the middle route mean that you should look for opportunities from the two corners and then make a sudden attack to the middle route to score. The body hit in the middle route is the common weakness for choppers; especially for the choppers who are relatively stable in returning heavy shots with the forehand and backhand, the middle route is the best breakthrough point.

(3) You can lift drive in straight lines and smash in crosscourt lines or lift drive in crosscourt lines and smash in straight lines. In the comparison of the two tactics, when lift driving in crosscourt lines and smashing in straight lines his lift drives will be more insured and steady; and although smashing in straight lines has a great menace but its technical difficulty is also bigger. When lift driving in straight lines and smashing in crosscourt lines it will be slightly more difficult for you to lift drive, but the difficulty of smashing

（4）拉一角为主，伺机扣杀，暴冲（用全力拉出的前冲弧圈球）扣杀自己特长线路或对方中路的战术。此战术在运用时，拉一角要选择对方削球不稳，旋转变化不强或攻势较弱的一面。这样容易寻找机会，避免被对方反攻。暴冲扣杀选择自己的特长线路，可以保证命中率。选择大力扣杀、拉冲对方中路，可增大对方顶重板的难度，加大扣杀拉冲的威胁。

（5）变化拉球的旋转强度、长短落点，伺机扣杀并使用拉攻战术。拉球技术比较过硬的选手常采用此战术，即在拉球过程中拉出强烈上旋和不转及侧旋弧圈球，用旋转变化来增加对方削球的难度。也可用拉球长短落点变化来创造机会，即先拉长球至对方端线处，迫使对方后退远削，再突然拉

in crosscourt lines will be reduced making a high hit ratio. Therefore, the use of these two tactics should be determined according to the opponents and the situation in the matches.

(4) You can lift drive to one corner primarily and await an opportunity to smash and attack with the all-out accelerated loop (the accelerated loop in full force) in your favorite line or to the middle route of the opponent. When using this tactic, you should select to lift drive to the corner of the side on which the opponent cannot chop steady and make changes of spin strongly or he (she) can do a weaker offensive. So it is easy to look for opportunities and refrain from the counter-offensive by the opponent. You should choose your favorite lines to smash and attack with the all-out accelerated loop, which can guarantee the hit ratio. Selecting the powerful smash and attack with the all-out accelerated loop to the middle route of the opponent can increase the difficulty of returning the heavy shots by the opponent, magnifying the menace of the powerful smash and the all-out accelerated loop.

(5) You can change the spin strength of the lift drive and placement of long and short awaiting an opportunity to smash and use the tactic of topspin drives. The players who have perfect mastery of lift drive techniques often adopt this tactic. Namely, in lift driving the ball you can lift drive a strong topspin, no-spin and sidespin loop, using spin changes to increase the difficulty for the opponent to chop. The placement changes of long and short can also be used to create opportunities. Namely, you can first lift drive a deep to the end line of the opponent forcing him back to do the long-range chop and then suddenly lift drive a drop shot to the right of the middle route (just outside the table); or you can first lift drive a heavy-spin loop which will

一板中路偏右的短球（刚出台），或先拉刚出台的高吊，再发力拉靠近端线的长球，从中寻找机会大力冲杀。

（6）拉搓、拉吊结合，伺机使用冲杀战术。此战术在运用时，可先用拉球结合突击迫使对方远离球台，然后用搓球或吊短球引其上前回接，再冲杀其中路及两大角，得到机会后连续扣杀。

4. 搓攻战术

搓攻战术是进攻型打法的辅助战术之一，也是与削球打法交战时的主要战术之一。此战术是利用搓球的旋转、落点变化为进攻创造条件。搓攻战术是进攻型打法必备的辅助战术，运用时搓球的板数不宜过多，以免陷入被动，一般搓一两板就要准备发起进攻。常用的前后左右搓攻战术有如下几种：

（1）先搓对方反手大角，再变直线，伺机抢攻战术。（如图4-17）

bounce just outside the table and then forcefully lift drive a deep to the end line, looking for an opportunity to attack with the all-out accelerated loop.

(6) You can use lift driving and pushing or lift driving and dropping shot in combination awaiting an opportunity to attack with the all-out accelerated loop. When using this tactic, you can first lift drive combined with a sudden attack to force the opponent away from the table and use the push or drop shot to seduce the opponent to come up to return afterwards, and then loop to his middle route and the two corners. After getting a chance you should smash continuously.

4. The tactic of pushing and attacking

The tactic of pushing and attacking is one of the auxiliary tactics for players of attacking play, and is one of the main tactics to cope with choppers. This tactic, which is the necessary auxiliary tactic of the attacking play, is to use the spin and placement changes of pushing to create conditions for attacking. When using the tactic, you should not push too much in case you fall into passiveness. Generally, you should be ready to attack after one or two push strokes. The several frequently-used tactics of pushing and attacking on all sides are as follows:

(1) You can first push to the backhand corner of the opponent and then change to a straight line awaiting an opportunity to attack.(As shown in fig.4-17)

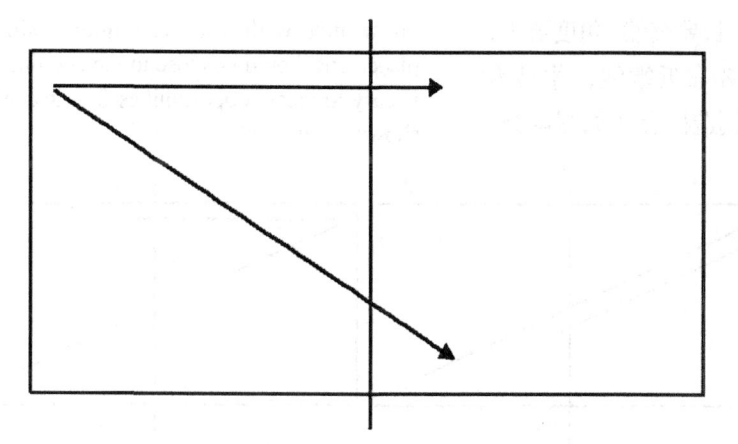

图 4-17 先搓对方反手大角、再变直线

Fig.4-17 First pushing to the backhand corner of the opponent and then changing to a straight line

此战术主要用于应对反手攻击力不强的选手,先搓对方的反手位大角,待其准备侧身或已把注意力放到反手时,变其正手伺机抢攻。

（2）以摆短为主,配合劈两大角长球,伺机抢攻战术。

此战术主要用于对付擅长抢攻长球的选手。目的是先用短球控制住对方,把对方引上来,再搓长出去,使其来不及抢攻或抢攻质量下降,寻机抢攻。运用此战术时要注意摆短的质量要高,弧线低又不出台,下旋旋转要强

This tactic is mainly used to cope with the players whose backhand attack is not strong. You should first push to the backhand corner of the opponent; when he(she) is about to move sideways or has been focusing on the backhand, you can change to his(her) forehand awaiting an opportunity to launch a preemptive attack.

(2) You can primarily drop shot and push deep to the two corners in combination awaiting an opportunity to attack.

This tactic is mainly used to cope with the players who are good at attacking a deep ball preemptively. The purpose is that you will first use the drop shot to control the opponent seducing him (her) to come up, and then push a deep ball out making it too late for him(her) to attack or the quality of his(her) attack reduced; subsequently you can look for an opportunity to launch a preemptive attack. When using this tactic, take note that you should make the drop-shot push with the high quality, low trajectory and strong backspin and make the deep push

烈,劈长要突然、角度要大,落点要靠近端线,才易为抢攻创造机会。(如图4-18)

all at once with a larger angle; besides, the placement should be close to the end line, which is easy to create opportunities for attacking. (As shown in fig.4-18)

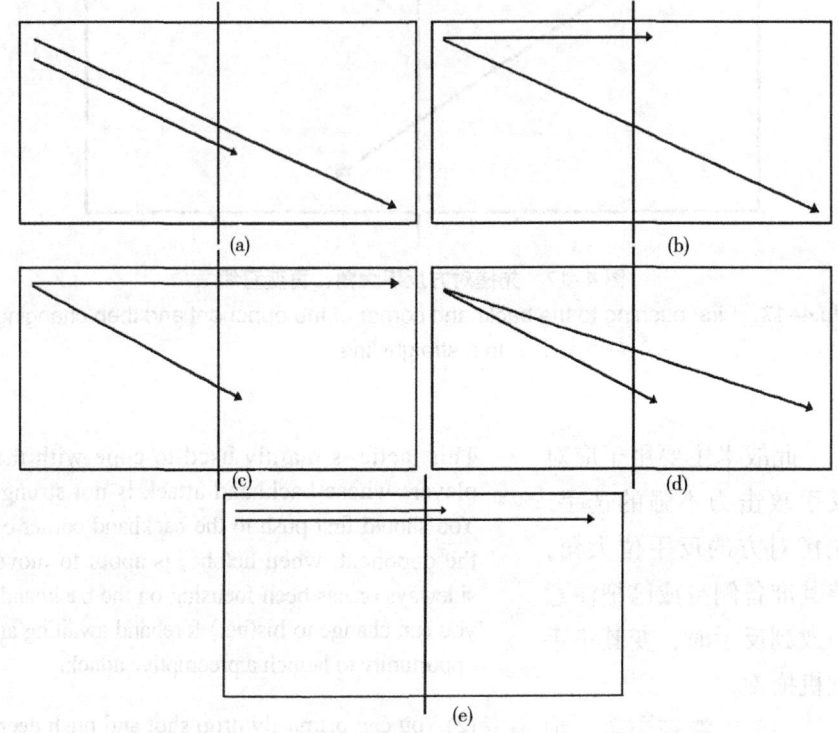

图 4-18 以摆短为主,配合劈两大角长球

Fig.4-18 Dropping shot primarily and pushing deep to the two corners in combination

(3)搓转与不转球,伺机采用抢攻战术。一般先以搓加转球为主,然后用相似的动作搓不转球,利用旋转的差别为抢攻创造机会,伺机抢攻。运用此战术时最好在旋转变化的基础上,再结合落点的变化效果更佳。

(3) You can make the heavy-spin push and no-spin push awaiting an opportunity to attack. Generally, you should first make the heavy-spin push primarily, and then make the no-spin push with similar action using the different spins to create opportunities for you to launch a preemptive attack. When using this tactic, you'd better make changes of placement in combination on the basis of spin changes, which will have a better effect.

（4）搓拉结合落点变化，伺机抢攻或反攻战术。此战术可分为以下三种情况：

①对搓中先拉一板，迫使对方打对攻，擅长打相持球的选手常用此战术。

②搓中突击，是正胶、生胶类进攻型选手的主要得分手段之一，可大胆运用。

③搓球至对方回球质量不高的一边，让其先把球拉起来，自己则准备反撕、反拉、反攻。

运用此战术一要具备反攻（反撕、反拉）的能力，二要提高搓球的质量，防止对方高质量的抢攻，造成自己的被动。

5. 削中反攻战术

这种战术主要靠稳健的削球，限制对方的进攻能力，为自己的反攻创造有利条件。它不仅增强了削球技术的生命力，也促进了攻防之间的积极转换。常用的削中反攻技术有以下几种。

(4) You can use pushing and lift driving combined with the placement change awaiting an opportunity to launch an attack or counterattack. This tactic can be divided into the three situations as follows:

① You can first make a topspin drive in exchanging pushes forcing the opponent to counterattack. The players who are good at playing the stalemate commonly use the tactic.

② You can make a sudden attack in exchanging pushes, which is one of the main scoring means of the attacking players who use the pips-out rubber or pips-out natural rubber; and you can be bold to use it.

③ You can push to the side of the opponent on which he(she) cannot return with high-quality ball making him(her) lift drive first, and yourself should get ready to counter fast flick, counter loop and counter attack.

Using this tactic, first you should have the ability to counterattack (counter fast flick, counter loop); second, you must improve the quality of pushing to guard against the high-quality attacking by the opponent causing yourself into passiveness.

5. The tactic of counterattacking during chops

This tactic depends mainly on the steady chops to restrict the attacking ability of the opponent and create the favorable conditions for yourself to counterattack, which has not only enhanced the vitality of the chopping technique but also promoted the positive transformation between offensive and defensive. The several commonly-used techniques of counterattacking in the course of chops are as follows:

（1）削转与不转球，伺机反攻。

一般是先削加转球，突然送出转与不转球，伺机上前反攻。旋转变化是削球选手争取主动的关键，从目前世界乒乓球技术的发展来看，没有旋转变化的削球是难以取胜的。

（2）逼两角，伺机反攻。

有先逼左角、再逼右角及先逼右角、再逼左角两种方法。对手右方攻势强的，先逼其左角；对手左方攻势强的，先逼其右角，使对方在大幅跑动中难以取得进攻机会。此战术若能和旋转变化相结合就更好。如先逼对方右角，再突变逼其左角，配合转与不转的变化，对方在来不及侧身攻时多以搓过渡，若判断不清就容易出高球或下网，削球选手可伺机反攻。

（3）削长短球，伺机反攻。

先连续削底线长球或中路追身球，然后结合旋

(1) You can make the heavy-spin and no-spin chops awaiting an opportunity to counterattack.

Commonly, you should first do the heavy-spin chops, and then suddenly put the heavy-spin and no-spin chops awaiting an opportunity to move forward to counterattack. The spin change is the key for choppers to gain the initiative. Seen from the perspective of the development of table tennis techniques at present in the world, it is difficult for choppers to win by chopping without spin changes.

(2) You can chop to the two corners awaiting an opportunity to counterattack.

There are two methods. You can first chop to the left corner and then chop to the right corner; or first chop to the right corner and then chop to the left corner. For the opponent who has a strong offensive on the right side, you should first chop to the left corner; and for the opponent who has a strong offensive on the left side, you should first chop to the right corner, making it difficult for him to obtain a chance in the big movement for attacking. If this tactic can be combined with spin changes, the effect will be better. For example, you can first chop to the right corner and then suddenly change to chop to the left corner cooperating with changes of spin and no-spin. When it is too late for the opponent to make a sideways attack, he will mostly push the ball as a transition. And if the judgment is incorrect it would be prone for the opponent to make a high ball or let it down the net, accordingly the chopper can await an opportunity to counterattack.

(3) You can use deep chops and a drop-shot chop to create an opportunity to counterattack.

You should first do deep chops to the end line or body hits to the middle route continuously and then do a drop-shot chop combined with

转变化，削一个短球，对手往往来不及反应，削球一方乘机实行反攻。

（4）接对方突击球时，逢斜变直、逢直变斜。

削球选手在接突击球时，即使接过去，也常遭对方连续攻击，最终失分。为在被动中争取主动，应采用"逢直变斜、逢斜变直"的战术，使对方不能站在固定的位置上击球，增加其连续进攻的难度。

（5）攻、挡、削结合，伺机反攻。

此战术适宜选择长胶球拍的直拍选手采用。在近台，用反手攻斜、直线后，伺机用正、反手抢攻。当对方轻拉时，可轻挡对方两大角，对方被迫改搓或将球轻轻托起后，迅速反攻；若对方发力拉时，一般以削球回接，伺机变挡或攻。这种打法在回球的旋转、落点、力量、节奏上皆有变化。

changes of spin. In most cases, it is too late for the opponent to respond; while the chopper can seize the opportunity to launch a counterattack.

(4) When returning the attacks from the opponent you can change the oncoming ball in the crosscourt line to the straight line and change the oncoming ball in the straight line to the crosscourt line.

When returning an attack from the opponent, even if you chop it back, you, as a chopper, will often meet with continual attacks by the opponent and be hard to avoid losing point ultimately. In order to gain the initiative in the passiveness, you should use the tactic in which you should change the crosscourt line to the straight line and change the straight line to the crosscourt line, making the opponent cannot hit the ball in a fixed position and increasing the difficulty for him(her) to make continual attacks.

(5) You can use attacks, blocks and chops in combination awaiting an opportunity to launch a counterattack.

This tactic is suitable for players of pen-hold grip who use the racket of long pips rubber, to use. At short court, you can first attack with backhand in crosscourt lines and straight lines and then await an opportunity to launch a preemptive attack with forehand or backhand. When the opponent drives lightly, you can lightly block the ball to the two corners of the opponent forcing him(her) to change to push or gently lift up the ball, and then you can quickly counterattack. When the opponent drives forcefully, generally, you should return it with a chop awaiting an opportunity to change to block or attack. In this kind of play all the spin, placement, power and rhythm of returning the ball have changes.

第二节
战术的运用

运用乒乓球战术一定要机动灵活，随机应变，针对不同的情况有的放矢，才会收到良好的效果，下面介绍几种不同情况下乒乓球战术的运用技巧。

1. 针对不同类型打法特点运用战术

乒乓球运动有各种不同类型的打法，每种类型打法都各有特点，运用战术时要针对双方的打法类型和各自特点进行分析，赛前制订出发球、发球抢攻阶段、相持阶段以及接发球阶段的具体战术。

例如，在应对以攻为主和以削为主的选手时，战术的运用就有所不同。在发球战术运用上，与应对以削为主的选手相比，应对以攻为主的选手时，发球更讲究控制好落点，发球要凶狠，要有更强的发球抢攻意识。因为稍有不慎，对手抢攻在先，

Section 2
Application of tactics

Application of table tennis tactics must be flexible and adaptable. You should play according to different situations and use tactics with a purpose, which will get a good effect. Here are several skills of using table tennis tactics in different circumstances.

1. Using tactics in allusion to characteristics of different typical styles

There are various different types of play in table tennis game and each type of play has its own characteristics. When using the tactics you should conduct an analysis in allusion to the playing styles and characteristics of both sides, and before competition you should work out the concrete tactics for the stages of serve, attack after service, counter attacks in a stalemate stage and serve receiving.

For example, the use of tactics is different in coping with players who play mainly with attacking and players who play primarily with chopping. In comparison to dealing with choppers, when coping with attackers you should pay more attention to a good controlling of the serve placement, and serve fiercely with the better consciousness for attack after service. If you is slightly careless the opponent will launch a preemptive attack ahead causing yourself into passiveness. However, choppers can also attack first but the utilization rate is far lower than that of attackers, so, the threat is relatively small. For another example, if the

自己就会陷于被动。而削球手虽然也有抢攻，但其使用率远低于攻球手。威胁相对较小。又如，当对手是不擅长侧身的两面攻（拉）选手时，可采用压中路调反手的战术；当对手虽为两面攻（拉）选手但遇中路来球习惯侧身攻者，可采用压中路调正手的战术；当对手是单面攻（拉）选手时，可视对手具体情况而定，当对方反手较强及侧身攻的意识较强时，采用调右压左的战术，当对手反手较弱时，可采用紧压对方反手，结合变线，伺机抢攻的战术。

2. 针对不同战局运用战术

运用乒乓球战术时，必须分析战局的发展。比赛刚开始时，双方都会不断变化打法，这就要求我们必须善于根据战局的需要及时采用相宜的战术。如削球对攻球手比赛，攻球手攻杀很凶时应怎么打？攻球手稳中带凶时该怎么办？攻球手打得手软，一味求稳，又该如何处理？

opponent is the player of two-winged attack (loop) who is not good at sideways attack (loop), you can use the tactic in which you should press to his(her) middle route and then move to the backhand position. And if the opponent is the player of two-winged attack (loop) who gets used to attack sideways when an oncoming ball is in the middle route, you can use the tactic in which you should press to his(her) middle route and then move to the forehand position. When opponent is the player of one-sided attack (loop), you should decide it according to the specific conditions of the opponent. If the opponent's backhand attack and the consciousness of sideways attack are stronger, you can use the tactic in which you should move him (her) to the forehand position and then press to the backhand location. And if the opponent's backhand attack is weaker, you can use the tactic in which you should firmly press to the backhand location of the opponent and combine with changing lines awaiting an opportunity to launch a preemptive attack.

2. Using tactics in allusion to different situations in a match

When using the table tennis tactics you must analyze the development of the situation in the matches. When the match begins, both sides will change their play style constantly. This requires that you must be good at adopting appropriate tactics according to the need of the situation in time. For instance, you as a chopper play against an attacker; when the attacker attacks very fiercely, how should you to play at this time? When the attacker seeks stability and attacks undecisively, what should you do? Seeking stability the attacker is irresolute when firmness is needed, and what should you deal with? If players fail to

运动员如果在战局转换时未能认清形势并改变打法，就很容易失利。当比赛打得顺手时，可适当加快节奏（如稍快些捡球、发球等），争取迅速结束战斗；当比赛打得不顺手时，则应适当放慢节奏，争取扭转场上的局势。

3. 针对不同比分运用战术

比分是比赛双方较量结果的现实标志，它直接影响运动员的心理状态，而运动员的心理状态又会直接影响其技术的发挥。运动员在比分领先时一般不主动变化，而对方往往会搏杀、拼抢，根据对方多发不转、上旋或长球的特点，我方应大胆挑打、进攻；根据对方侧身多的打法，我方应及时变线调动对方；根据对方相持中发力多的特点，我方应加强控制，增加对方发力攻难度，并力争抢先上手，灭掉对方的威风。当对方比分领先时，我方应表现出一种大无畏的精神，坚定信心，冷静分析，抓住主要矛盾，果断改变战术。

see clearly the situation and change their play when the transformation of situations appears in the match, it is prone to lead to failure. When playing well in the game you can speed up the game tempo appropriately (such as picking up the ball and serving a little faster, etc.) trying to end the match quickly. When playing with difficulties, you should slow down the game rhythm properly trying hard to reverse the situation in the match.

3. Using tactics in allusion to different scores

The point score is the real symbol which shows the result of competition between both the sides and directly affects the mental state of players; moreover, the player's mental state will directly affect the techniques play. When your score is in the lead generally, you should not change initiatively; and yet, the opponent will tend to fight and kill desperately. If the opponent has the characteristics of making more serves of no spin, topspin and the deep ball, you should be bold to flip and attack. If the opponent plays more sideways, you should change lines to move him(her) in time. And if the opponent often puts forth strength in a sustained rally, you should strengthen the control to increase the difficulty for the opponent to attack forcefully, and strive to take actions first destroying his(her) might. When the opponent's score is in the lead, you should show a fearless spirit, proceed with confidence and calmly analyze the problems; meanwhile, grasp the main contradiction to change tactics decisively.

有时，只要处理好某一板球（如接好小球），或是稍微改变一下回球落点（如原来打反手太多，现以打正手为主），就可能扭转战局。要充分利用发球的机会，大胆抢攻，这是缩小分差的关键环节。当运动员双方实力相当，技、战术发挥和使用也在同等水平上，比分交替上升，没有大的起伏，形成相互克制的抗衡局面时，双方一时均无摆脱困境的能力和打破僵局的可能，此刻比分给双方的压力是同等沉重的。在这紧张、对抗的阶段，打好相持球最为重要的是意志要坚定，也就是取胜的信念要强烈，贯彻战术要坚决，技术动作出手要果断，意志品质要顽强。同时，还要及时准确地寻找对方的弱点，发现对方的意图，以狠攻弱点来打开局面，而对方此时的弱点大都来自心理上的脆弱。

4. 针对规则运用战术

（1）现行的 11 分制要求运动员进入状态一定要

Sometimes as long as you handles a certain stroke well (such as returning an oncoming ball well) or slightly changes the placement of next return (for example, you formerly hits to the backhand position too much, and now you primarily hit to the forehand position), you may turn the table. You should take full advantage of the opportunity to serve and launch a preemptive attack boldly, which is a key link of narrowing the scoring gap. When the players of both sides are well-matched in strength, in the meantime, their play and use of techniques and tactics are also on the same level; and the match goes point for point, no big ups and downs, forming the situation of mutual restraint and contending against each other; both sides at that time have no ability to break the deadlock, at this moment the score equally gives a heavy pressure to both sides. And in this period of tension and confrontation, the most important thing is the strong will for playing well in a sustained rally; and namely, you should have the strong thought of winning and implement tactics resolutely; at the same time, you should do the movements of technique decisively with the tenacious will and quality. And meanwhile, you should find the weaknesses and intentions of the opponent timely and accurately; and then open up a new prospect with resolute attacks to his weaknesses. However, the opponent's weaknesses are mostly from the psychological vulnerability at this time.

4. Using tactics in allusion to regulations

(1) The current 11-score system demands that athletes must get into the state fast. At

快，开局（前4分称为开局）就应"拼命"，打个人特长，以自己的战术变化为主，重视技术的严密性。减少无谓失误，争取开局领先。5~8分为中局，双方都已对对方有所了解，应实施最有效的战术。具体可采用以长打短、以长打长或以短打短的战术，力争取得局部优势，可以适当打得凶狠些，争取打出一两个高潮，为获得本局的胜利打下基础。9分以后称为收局或末局，应根据场上情况决定采用大胆搏杀还是灵活巧妙的打法。11分制打到9:10或10:10的比分特别多，所以，应特别注意对此类关键球的处理。

　　总的来说，11分制对精力的要求很高，特别强调对每个球的算计。运用战术时必须重视发球及战术的多变，这就要求运动员要格外珍惜发球机会，充分利用好发球权，扬长避短，避实就虚。由于每一轮2个发球不容易配套变化，因此可将一局中的发球联系起来综合考虑，

the opening (the period of the first four points is called the opening) you should "put up a desperate fight" and play your special skills, in the meantime, give priority to your tactical changes and attach great importance to the technical rigor. And you should also reduce needless errors striving for leading score at the opening. The period of 5 ~ 8 points is called the middle game at which both the sides have gained some understanding for each other, so, you should carry out the most effective tactics. You can concretely use the tactics in which you can return a short ball with a long shot and play long shots against long shots, or use a short shot against a drop shot. In brief, you can properly play more fiercely striving to achieve partial advantage, and try hard to play one or two climaxes so as to lay the foundation for the winning of the game. It is called the ending of the game after 9 points, in which you should decide whether to adopt the bold and adventurous playing style or the flexible and clever playing style according to the situations in the game. In the 11-score system, the point scores of 9:10 or 10:10 appear frequently; therefore, you should pay special attention to handling this type of game winning shots.

In summary, the 11-score system has a very high demand for energy; and you should play with special emphasis on the careful consideration for each ball. When using the tactics, you must attach more importance to the change of serves and tactics, which requires you to especially cherish opportunity to serve; and make full use of the right to serve. And you should enhance your advantage and avoid your disadvantage and keep clear of the opponent's main force and strike at the weak points. It is not easy to form a complete set of changes because there are only two chances to serve in each round; so, you

即根据对方的特点，决定一局中发球的大体变化规律，如发球的种类、路线、配套变化等，再根据场上的具体情况，灵活运用。

（2）针对大球运用战术。改用 40$^+$ 毫米的大球后，球的旋转和速度减弱，回球率提高，这样，相持阶段的战术变化能力将成为得分的关键因素之一。相持是一种暂时的平衡状态，谁首先打破这种平衡，谁就能先占据主动。这对运动员根据对手的情况而灵活多变地调整和运用战术的能力提出了更高的要求。在旋转、速度变慢后，抢先主动发力和击球落点变化是战术运用的主要方面。另外，在战术的具体运用上，靠单一的战术或特长战术获胜的比重降低，而接发球抢攻战术，左推右攻等的地位和作用明显提高。

should give a comprehensive consideration for the serves together in the game. Namely, you should determine the varying pattern of serves in a game on the whole according to the characteristics of the opponent, such as the types, the lines of serves and a complete set of serve changes; and then use them flexibly on the basis of the specific circumstance in the game.

(2) You can use tactics in allusion to the big ball. After using the big ball of 40$^+$ mm, the spin and speed of the ball are reduced, but the return rate is increased; as thus, the ability of tactic changes in the stalemate stage will become one of the key factors for scoring. Being locked in a stalemate is the balanced state which is temporary; and anyone who first to break the balance, will be able to first take the initiative. Therefore, higher requirements are put forward for players' ability to adjust and use tactics flexibly according to the opponent's conditions. After the spin and speed become slower, forestalling to give force and changing the placement of hitting are the main aspects of tactical use. Furthermore, for the concrete application in tactics, the proportion of winning victory which relies on a single tactic or the tactics of strong points has dropped. And the status and role of the tactics such as the attack of service return and the backhand block with forehand attack, etc. are obviously improved.

5. 针对接发球运用战术

首先要在清楚对方发球旋转的情况下，在接发球的手段上突破以摆为主的被动式接发球模式，建立以进攻手段为主（如：采用挑打、抢拉以及台内拧拉等进攻手段来接发球）、主动劈长、摆短为辅的新模式，争取抢占先机或直接得分。由于接发球技术在现行的规则里变得越来越重要，所以接发球要实现"一体化"。一体化指的是接发球后以及下一板的衔接要形成一体，才算是一个完整的接发球技术，接发球手段和下一板的衔接哪一个环节出现问题都不是好的接发球。接发球战术有以下几种：

（1）一般旋转的来球，只要一出台，或者能够抢上手的半出台球，以抢拉对方的反手或中路偏右处为主，形成主动拉冲局面。

（2）来球下旋强烈，无论是正手位还是反手位，应先抢拉一板加转（高吊）弧圈球，再伺机冲对方的弱点。

5. Using tactics in allusion to serve receiving

First of all you should know the spin of serves by the opponent, and then you should break through the stereotype of passive receiving in which the techniques of controlling are used primarily, regarding the means of service receiving. What is more, you should create a new receiving pattern in which the means of offensive are used primarily (for instance, return serves with the means of offensive such as the flip, first loop and over-the-table twist drive, etc.) and the deliberate deep push and drop-shot push are used as assistance, striving for first chance or score directly. In the current rules the techniques of service returning get more and more important, therefore, "integration" should be implemented for service returning. Integration means that service receiving and the next stroke after it should be formed as a whole, which can be called an integral technique of service receiving. It is not good service receiving whether the receiving method or the connection of the next stroke goes wrong. There are several tactics of service receiving as follows:

(1) For an oncoming ball of ordinary spin, as long as it bounces off the table or just off the table, which you can get in, you should loop first primarily to the backhand position or the right of the middle route of the opponent forming a situation of active looping.

(2) For an oncoming ball of heavy backspin, whether it is in the forehand position or backhand position, you should first do a heavy-spin loop (high loop) and then await an opportunity to fast loop to the opponent's weaknesses.

（3）以反手快拨或快推控制落点，形成对拉相持局面。

（4）以加转快搓近网短球，结合搓两底线长球或反手大角度后抢拉。

只有通过积极主动、灵活多变的战术运用，才能做到真正意义上的抢先上手，争取在前三板、前五板得分或进入主动相持阶段。

(3) You can control the placement of your return with the backhand fast flick or fast block creating a stalemate of counter looping.

(4) You can do a drop shot with fast push of heavy spin and in combination push the deep ball to the end line of the two corners or to the opponent's backhand position with a large angle; and then loop first.

Only through active and flexible application of tactics can you first take actions in its true sense, and endeavor to score in the first three to five strokes or do all they can to get into the stage of active stalemate.

第五章
乒乓球运动的双打技术

Chapter 5
Doubles techniques of table tennis

双打在乒乓球比赛中占有重要的地位，它可以培养团结协作的精神，能够吸引更多的人参与乒乓球运动。双打配对要求同伴之间合作默契，并能互相鼓励，彼此谅解。在技术上要能互为补充，共同发挥特长。

第一节
双打的规则与配对

1. 双打规则

双打比赛竞赛方法和比赛规则与单打基本相同，但双打在发球、接发球及击球的顺序上有特殊的规定。乒乓球台面的中央，划有一条3毫米宽的白线，称为中线，把台面均等地分为左、右两个半区。双打比赛时，右半区为发球区。发球时，球必须先落到本方的发球区或中线上，然后落到对方的发球区或中线上，否则判为发球方失分。双打第一局发球的一方，应先确定第一发球员，而接发球的一方，可任意确定第一接球员，然后按规定的次序，轮流交换发球和接发球。此后各局先发球的一方，可以任意确定第一发球

Doubles holds an important position in table tennis matches, which can cultivate the spirit of solidarity and collaboration for players and attract more and more people to take part in table tennis sports. The pairing of doubles requires the cooperation of tacit understanding between partners who can encourage and forgive each other and on the techniques, complement each other to play their special skills jointly.

Section 1
Rules and pairing of doubles

1. The rules for doubles

The competition method and rules for the doubles game are basically the same with that of singles; but the doubles game has special provisions for the sequence of serve, return of serve and hitting the ball. A white line of 3 mm wide is in the centre of the table-board that is called as the center line, by which the playing surface is equally divided into two half courts of the left and the right. In the doubles match the right half court is the service area. When serving, the ball must first fall into the service area or on the center line of the server, and then bounce to the service area or on the center line of the opponent. Otherwise, it will be judged as losing point by the serving side. In the doubles match the serving side should choose the first server in the first game, while the receiving side can choose the first receiver at will; and then exchange serve and receive in turn according to the specified order. Hereafter, in each game the side of first serving can determine the first server at will; while for the receiving

员，而接发球的一方，则必须由前一局与之相对应的发球员来接发球。决胜局交换方位时，发球次序不变，但接发球一方应交换接球员的次序，这些规定是根据比赛双方机会均等的原则作出的。

side, the serve must be received by the corresponding server in the preceding game. When changing ends in the deciding game, the service order remains the same; but the receiving side should exchange the order of the receivers. These rules are made out on the basis of the principle which provides equal opportunity for both sides of competition.

2. 双打的配对

配对是打好双打的重要条件之一，一个好的配对应该有利于运动员灵活地交换位置，缩小走动范围，避免连续击球中的碰撞，并有利于合理运用战术，使技术特长得到发挥（如图5-1）。较理想的配对有以下几种。

2. The pairing of doubles

Pairing is one of the important conditions for playing doubles well. A good pairing should help players to exchange positions flexibly and shrink the moving range to avoid collisions in continuous shots. In the meantime, it is conducive to using tactics reasonably making the players give full play to their technique specialties (As shown in fig. 5-1). There are several ideal pairings as follows:

图 5-1 双打的配对
Fig. 5-1 The pairing of doubles

（1）一名左手握拍和一名右手握拍的攻球手相配。这种配对有利于减少走动范围，并充分发挥正手攻球的威力。

（2）一名弧圈球选手和一名快攻选手配对。两人一前一后，一快一转，互为补充。

（3）一名直拍正胶和一名直拍反胶选手配对。

（4）两名削球手配对。最好是一个站位稍前，擅长逼角；另一个站位稍远，擅长旋转变化。或者两人都是稳健型削球手，但有较强的反攻能力。

（5）一名使用两面不同性能球拍的选手和一名使用常规球拍的选手配对。前者发挥球拍的不同性能，不断变化球的旋转性质，为后者的进攻创造条件。

第二节 双打的站位、步伐与战术

1. 双打的站位

站位是指双打发球或

(1) A left-hander attacker can be paired with a right-hander attacker. This kind of pairing helps reduce players' moving range and give full play to the powers of forehand attack.

(2) A looping player can be paired with a quick attacker, the two players, of whom one is in front and the other is in the back meanwhile, one plays fast and the other plays with rotation, which can complement each other.

(3) A pen-hold-grip player who uses a pips-out rubber racket can be paired with a pen-hold-grip player who uses an inverted rubber racket, which can complement each other.

(4) Two choppers compose a pairing. The best is that one player who is good at pressing to the corners of the opponent stands slightly in front; and the other player who is good at spin changes stands a little bit far from the table. Or both players are steady choppers, but both have a strong ability of counterattack.

(5) A player using a racket of two different properties can be paired with the other player using a conventional racket. And the former can give play to the different properties of the racket to change spins of the ball constantly creating the conditions for the latter to attack.

Section 2 Formation, footwork and tactics of doubles

1. The formation of doubles

The formation refers to the positional relation

接发球时，配对的双方彼此间的位置关系。只有站位合理，才能迅速移动，让位方便，避免冲撞，有利于发挥个人的特点（如图 5-2）。常用的站位方式有以下几种。

between both players of the pair when serving or receiving in the doubles game. Only a sound formation can make players move quickly and give way conveniently avoiding collisions; at the same time it is conducive to giving full play to the specialties of individuals (As shown in fig. 5-2). The followings are several commonly-used formations.

图 5-2 双打的站位
Fig. 5-2 The formation of doubles

（1）平行站位。

发球方：发球员站位偏右，让出 3/4 的位置给同伴。

接球方：这一站位方式多为一左一右直拍的进攻型选手采用，进攻型选手用反手接发球时也常采用这一站位方式。

(1) Side by side formation.

The serving side: the server should stand on the right making a space of 3/4 to the partner.

The receiving side: this kind of formation is mostly used by the pairing of pen-hold grip attacking players, of whom one is a left-hander, the other is a right-hander. When attacking players return serves with the backhand they mostly use the formation.

（2）前后站位。

发球方：常为削球型选手采用，发球员站位稍前，其同伴站位居中稍后。

接球方：进攻型选手用正手接发球时站位近台偏中，有利于正手进攻，其同伴稍后错位站立；削球型选手无论以正反手接发球均以前后站位为宜。

2. 双打的步伐

双打步伐的要求是击球后迅速移动，避免对方打追身球；移动时不能妨碍同伴击球，站位尽量接近下次击球最有利的位置。常用的移动方法有以下几种。

（1）"八"字形移动。

左手执拍与右手执拍的直拍进攻型选手配对，多采用此走位法。两人击球后均向自己反手侧移动，这样既确保了同伴的击球空位，又有利于发挥自己正手攻球的优势。（如图5-3）

(2) Front-and-back formation.

The serving side: this kind of formation is mostly used by the pairing of choppers, in which the server stands slightly in front with his(her) partner standing a little bit behind in the middle.

The receiving side: when an attacking player returns a serve with the forehand, he(she) should stand close to the table slightly in the middle, which is conducive to the forehand attack; and his(her) partner should stand slightly behind in the staggered position. For the chopping players whether they return serves with the forehand or backhand, it is advisable to use the front-and-back formation.

2. The footwork of doubles

The footwork of doubles requires that players quickly move after hitting the ball avoiding a body hit stroked by the opponent; and when moving, a player cannot hamper the partner from hitting the ball. So, the players' location should be as far as possible close to the most favorable position for the next shot. The followings are several commonly-used movement patterns.

(1) The movement pattern of the Chinese character "八".

The movement pattern is more adapted by the pairing of pen-hold grip attacking players, of whom one is a left-hander, the other is a right-hander. Both players should move to their own backhand side after hitting the ball, which can ensure the room for the partner to hit the ball and as well help his(her) own play the advantages of the forehand attack. (As shown in fig. 5-3)

图 5-3 "八"字形移动

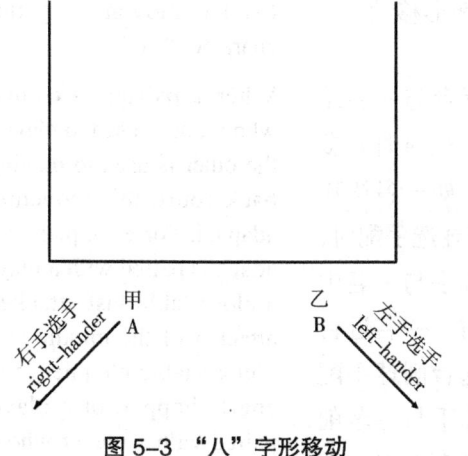

Fig. 5-3　The movement pattern of the Chinese character "八"

（2）环形移动。

两名皆是右手执拍的选手配对时，多采用此移位法。（如图 5-4）

(2) The movement pattern of a ring shape.

When a pairing is composed of two right-handers this movement pattern is more adapted. (As shown in fig. 5-4)

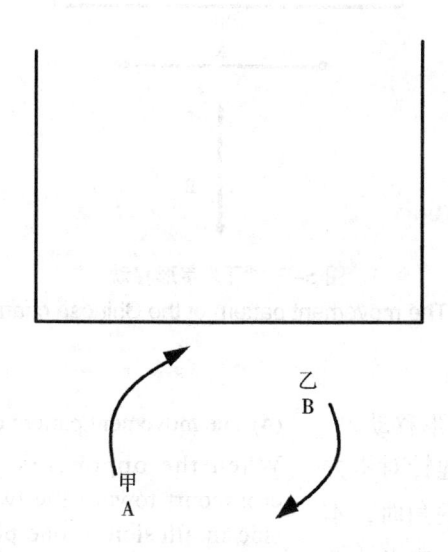

图 5-4　环形移动

Fig. 5-4　The movement pattern of a ring shape

（3）"丁"字形移动。

一名站位近台与一名站位中远台的选手配对时，多采用此走位法。如一名快攻选手与一名弧圈球选手配对，一名近台快攻选手与一名中远台攻球手配对，一名近台削球手与一名远台削球手配对，一名快攻选手与一名削攻结合打法选手配对时，多采用此移位法。（如图5-5）

(3) The movement pattern of the Chinese character " 丁 ".

When a pairing is composed of players of whom one is used to playing in the short court, the other is used to playing in the middle and back court, this movement pattern is more adapted. For examples, when a player of fast attack is paired with a player of looping, when a close-table fast attacker is paired with an attacker of the middle and back court, when a close-table chopper is paired with a back-court chopper, or a player of fast attack is paired with a player who combines chopping with attacking, all of them will mostly use this movement pattern. (As shown in fig. 5-5)

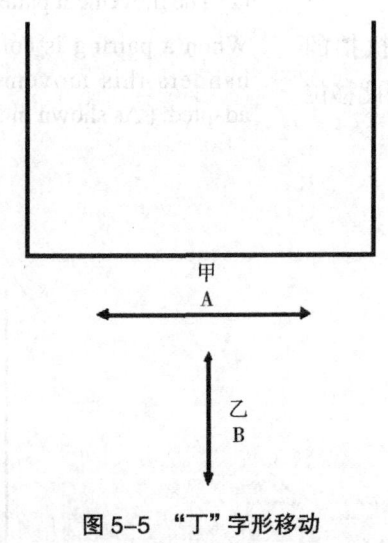

图 5-5 "丁"字形移动

Fig. 5-5 The movement pattern of the Chinese character "丁"

（4）"∞"字形移动。

对方有意识地针对本方一名选手交叉打两角时，本方可采用"∞"字形移位路线。（如图5-6）

(4) The movement pattern of "∞" shape.

When the opponents purposefully hit crosscourt toward the two corners of your side in allusion to one player of your pair, you can adopt the moving line of "∞" shape. (As shown in fig. 5-6)

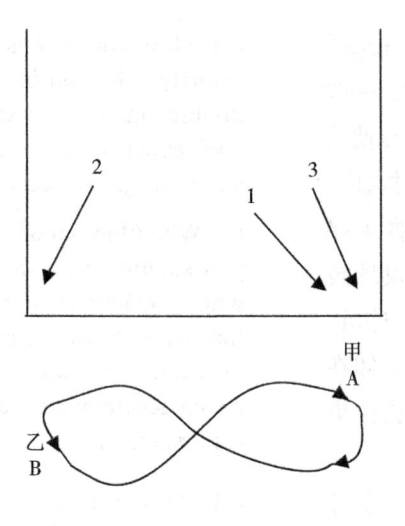

图 5-6 "∞"字形移动
Fig. 5-6 The movement pattern of "∞" shape

3. 双打的战术

由于双打是两人协同作战，各人的技术特长和风格不同，因此在战术运用上比单打要复杂一些。除了要很好地研究对方的特点外，还要根据配对的两人的特点来确定战术运用策略。在双打比赛中，先发制人，力争主动的战术思想尤为突出，往往在前三板中就决定一分球的胜负。即使是以削为主的配对，也应贯彻积极防御的思想，力争以旋转和落点的变化控制对方，伺机组织进攻。下面是几种常用的战术。

3. The tactics of doubles

Because the doubles game is a cooperative operation of two players who have the different technique specialties and playing styles; so, the tactical use is more complicated than that of singles. In addition to studying the opponents' characteristics very well, you should determine the strategies of tactical application according to the features of the two players in their pairing. In the doubles match the tactical concept is particularly outstanding, in which you should forestall the opponents and do all you can to gain the initiative; and in most cases you will decide the outcome of the ball in the first three strokes. Even if the players in the pair who mainly use chopping, should also carry out the idea of active defense and strive for controlling the opponents by the changing the spin and placement of returns, awaiting an opportunity to build up an attack. Here are several common tactics.

（1）双打抽签时，优先选择接发球。双打比赛时，一般应优先选择接发球，以便选择有利的发球、接发球次序。

（2）当对方选择了接发球时，应由我方发球技术好的选手为第一发球员，以争取开局的主动。如在混双比赛中，一般选择男选手为第一发球员。

（3）发球抢攻：发球者发球时，可用手势暗示同伴要发出什么球，以做好抢攻的准备。另外，同伴有时也可主动暗示发球者发什么球，直接为自己下一板抢攻或抢拉制造机会。双打的发球抢攻比单打难度大，要敢于在发球后果断抢攻，同时又要做好对方接发球抢攻后自己积极防御的准备。一旦难以上手，不要盲目扣杀，可用中等力量打对方的弱点；或控制一板，为同伴创造下一板抢攻的机会。

① 可以发近网下旋转与不转球或侧上、侧下旋球进行抢攻。要特别注意发球落点，对于对方右手接发球者，多发中路近网和中路底线区域，对方如

(1) When drawing lots for the doubles game, priority selection is service return. In the doubles match you should generally give preference to return of service, in order to select an advantageous order of serving and receiving.

(2) When the opponents chose to receive, you should select the player in your pair, whose technique of serve is better, as the first server so as to strive for the initiative at the start. For example, in the mixed doubles match generally the male player is chosen as the first server.

(3) Attack after service: Before serving, the server can give a hint by a gesture to tell the partner what kind of ball will be served, so as to let him(her) get ready for a preemptive attack. In addition, the partner sometimes can also actively give a gesture to tell the server what kind of ball should be served to directly create an opportunity for him(her) to play the next stroke of preemptive attack or loop. The attack after service in the doubles game is more difficult than that of singles; and you should dare to attack decisively after service, in the meantime, you should have the preparation for an active defense after a service return attack by the opponent. Once it is hard to take actions you should not smash blindly; you can hit to the weaknesses of the opponents with a medium strength or make a stroke of controlling to create an opportunity for the next preemptive attack by your partner.

①The pairing can do short serves of backspin and no-spin to the net zone of the opponents or do the serves of side topspin and side backspin to launch a preemptive attack. And you should pay special attention to the placement of serves. For the right-handed receiver of the opponents, you should do more short serves to the net

是左手接发球者，应多发右近网和右大角度球。（如图 5-7）

zone and the serves deep to the end line in the middle route; and for the left-handed receiver you should do more short serves to the net zone and the deep serves with large angle on the right side. (As shown in fig. 5-7)

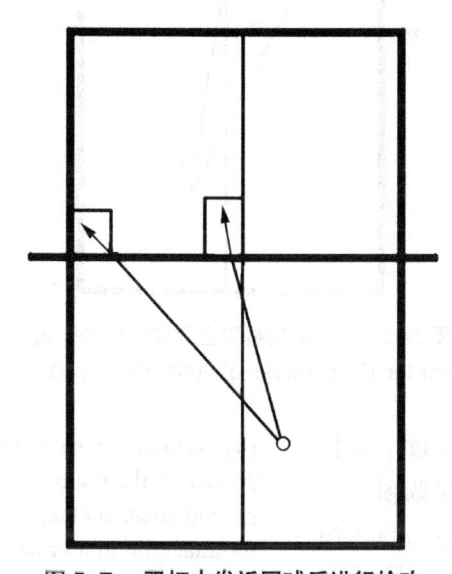

图 5-7　双打中发近网球后进行抢攻
Fig. 5-7　Attack after the short serves in the doubles game

②偶尔发右侧上旋奔球进行抢攻，落点是：对方是右手接发球者，多发中路底线球；对方是左手接发球者，多发右方底线球。（如图 5-8）

② The pairing can occasionally serve the deep right-side topspin to carry out a preemptive attack, and pay attention to the placement. For the right-handed receiver of the opponents, you should do more serves to the end line in the middle route; and for the left-handed receiver you should do more serves to the end line on the right side. (As shown in fig. 5-8)

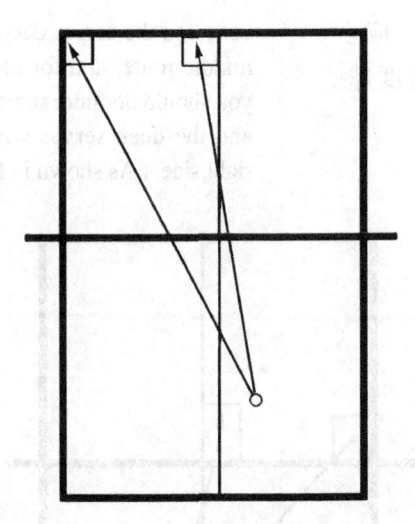

图 5-8　双打中发右侧上旋奔球后进行抢攻

Fig. 5-8　Attack after the deep serves of right-side topspin in the doubles game

（4）接发球抢攻：双打的接发球应特别强调积极主动，力争抢攻，或为同伴创造抢攻机会，同时注意同伴间的配合。（如图 5-9）

(4) Attack on serve: When returning a service in the doubles game you should lay special stress on taking the initiative to aim for attacking first or creating an opportunity for your partner to attack. And at the same time you should also pay attention to the cooperation between partners. (As shown in fig. 5-9)

图 5-9　接发球抢攻配合

Fig. 5-9　Cooperation of attacking after receiving a serve in the doubles game

假设对方发我右方近网球，如何接发球？

①若对方两名选手皆是右手横拍，则回至对方左、右两个大角 A、B 处，或回至接球者中路追身 C 处。（如图 5-10）

You can assume that the opposite party does a short serve to the right side of your party; how to return it?

①If the opponents are both right-handers of shake-hand grip, you should return the ball to the point A and the point B at the two corners of the opposite party or return to the receiver a body-hit at the point C in the middle route. (As shown in fig. 5-10)

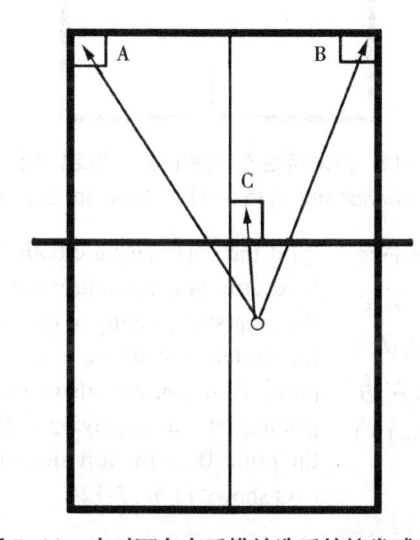

图 5-10 应对两名右手横拍选手的接发球位置
Fig. 5-10 The service return to two right-handers of shake-hand grip

②若对方两名选手皆是左手横拍，也可回至对方左右两角 A、B；或回至接球者中路追身 C、D。（如图 5-11）

②If the opponents are both left-handers of shake-hand grip, you should return the ball to the point A and the point B at the two corners of the opposite party. And you can also return a body-hit of the receiver to the point C and the point D in the middle route. (As shown in fig. 5-11)

图 5-11　应对两名左手横拍选手的接发球位置

Fig. 5-11　The service return to two left-handers of shake-hand grip

③若对方两名选手皆是右手直拍，可搓、摆至对方中线左侧近网 A 处；或搓、撇、挑至对方左边大角度 B 处。（如图 5-12）

③ If the opponents are both right-handers of pen-hold grip, you can return the ball with pushing or the drop-shot pushing to the point A in the net zone on the left side of the center line of the opposite party. And you can also return the ball with the pushing, the feint playing or flip by large angle to the point B on the left side of the opposite party. (As shown in fig. 5-12)

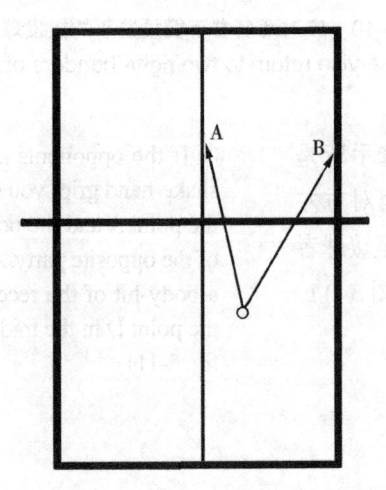

图 5-12　应对两名右手直拍选手的接发球位置

Fig. 5-12　The service return to two right-handers of pen-hold grip

④若对方两名选手皆是横拍，一左一右，如是左手接球，可攻击对方左边大角度 A 处；如是右手接球，可攻击对手中路追身 B、C 处，也可摆短控制到 D 处。（如图 5-13）

④ If the opponents are two players of shake-hand grip, of whom one is the left-hander and the other is the right-hander; when the left-hander receives the ball, you can attack with large angle to the point A on the left side of the opposite party. When the right hander receiving the ball, you can hit a body-hit of the receiver to the point B or the point C in the middle route; and you can also hit a drop short controlling the ball to the point D. (As shown in fig. 5-13)

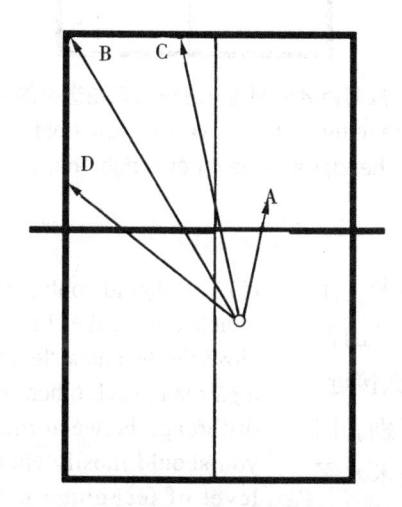

图 5-13　应对两名分别为一左一右横拍选手的接发球位置

Fig. 5-13　The service return to two players of shake-hand grip, of whom one is left-hander and the other is right-hander

⑤若对方两名选手皆是直拍，一左一右，可回接至对方左边线近网 A、B 处；或接至下一位击球者追身 C、D 处。（如图 5-14）

⑤ If the opponents are two players of pen-hold grip, of whom one is the left-hander and the other is the right-hander; you can return the ball to the point A or the point B which are close to the net on the left-side line, or return to the point C or the point D, which are the body-hit positions of the next striker. (As shown in fig. 5-14)

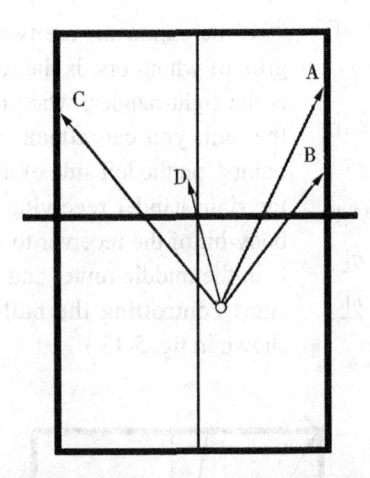

图 5-14　应对两名分别为一左一右直拍选手的接发球位置

Fig. 5-14　The service return to two players of pen-hold grip, of whom one is left-hander and the other is right-hander

（5）控制较强者，主攻较弱者：双打配对的两人无论技术水平多么接近，其攻击力总会有区别。因而大多选择对方技术水平相对较低，攻击力相对较弱者作为主要攻击对象。想要选准主要的攻击对象，事先必须了解清楚对方的技术情况及打法特点。

（6）紧盯一角，突袭另一角：紧盯对方一角，把对方两人挤在一边，迫使他们在一角匆忙交换击球位置，在此过程中，突然袭击对方的另一角，打出机会球，进行扣杀。

(5) You should control the stronger and mainly attack the weaker. In doubles no matter how close the technical level of the two players in a pair is to each other, there will be always the difference between their attacks. Therefore, you should mostly choose the player, whose level of technique is relatively lower and attacking force is comparatively weaker as the main object of attack. In order to choose the main object of attack, you must find out the technical conditions and playing characteristics of the opponents in advance.

(6) You can press fixedly to one corner and then launch a surprise attack to the other corner. You can first press fixedly to one corner forcing the two players of the opposite party to huddle in one side and hastily exchange positions of hitting the ball around the corner. And in the process, you can suddenly attack the other corner of the opponents making a chance to smash.

（7）交叉攻两角或长短结合：把右手握拍向左移动的选手调到右边去，把左手握拍向右移动的选手调到左边来，把近台攻的选手挤到后面去，把中台进攻的选手诱到近台来。这样，既打乱了对方的基本站位和基本跑位方法，破坏了对方的协调配合，也能为扣杀创造机会。

（8）各施所长：双打和单打一样，在制订作战方案和采用战术时的基本方略是能充分发挥两人之所长。如果配对的两名选手，一人防守较好，一人进攻较强，一般由防守好的人来抵挡对方的强者，进攻强的人攻击对方弱者，以突破对方的防线。

（9）有针对性地将球击向对方两名选手的不同弱点，使其处于被动局面，并伺机抢攻。

（10）利用落点的变化将速度、旋转相结合,控制、调动对方，争取主动。

(7) You can attack the two corners crossways or play long and short balls in combination. You can transfer the right-hander who moves to the left, to the right side, and transfer the left-hander who moves to the right, to the left side. You can also press the close-table attacker to the middle and back court or seduce the middle-court attacker to the short court. In this way, you can disorganize the opponents' basic formation and basic footwork and damage the coordinative cooperation of the opponents. And at the same time, you will be able to create opportunities to smash.

(8) Each player of a pair should play personal strength. The doubles game is same as singles. When making the match plan and using tactics, the basic strategy is that you should give full play to personal strengths of the two players in your pair. If the two players compose your pair, one of whom is better skilled in defense and the other is stronger in attack; generally, you should use the player who is better skilled in defense to fend against the stronger player in the opposite party; and the player who is stronger in attack undertakes attacking the weaker of the opposite party so as to break through the opponents' defensive line.

(9) You can purposefully hit the ball to the different weaknesses of the two players in the opposite party making them into a passive situation, and await an opportunity to launch a preemptive attack.

(10) You can also use the change of placement in combination with the changes of speed and spin to control and move the opponents in order to gain the initiative.

第六章
乒乓球运动的比赛知识

Chapter 6
Knowledge of table tennis game

第一节
乒乓球竞赛规则简介

1. 乒乓球比赛常用术语

（1）回合：球处于比赛状态的一段时间。

（2）球处比赛状态：从发球时，球被有意向上抛起前静止在不执拍手掌上的最后一瞬间，持续到该回合被判得分或重发球。

（3）重发球：不予判分的回合。

（4）一分：判分的回合。

（5）执拍手：正握着球拍的手。

（6）不执拍手：未握着球拍的手。

（7）击球：用握在手中的球拍或执拍手手腕以下部分触球。

（8）阻挡：自对方击球后，如果在台面上方或正向比赛台面方向运动的球，在尚未触及本方台区、也未越过端线之前，即触及本方运动员或其穿戴的任何物品。

（9）发球员：在一个回合中，首先击球的运动员。

Section 1
Introduction to the rules of table tennis game

1. Common terms of table tennis game

(1) "A rally" means a period of time during which the ball is in play.

(2) "The ball in play" means a period of time which is from the last instant when the ball rests in the palm of the free hand before it is thrown up intentionally at the beginning of service till the rally is determined as scoring or let.

(3) "Let" means the rally of which the result is not scored.

(4) "Point" means the rally of which the result is scored.

(5) "The racket hand" means the hand which is holding the racket.

(6) "The free hand" means the hand which is not holding the racket.

(7) "Striking the ball" means that a player hits the ball with the racket held in the hand or the part below the wrist of the racket hand.

(8) "Obstruct" means that after the opponent hitting the ball, you or anything you wear touch it when the ball is travelling above your playing surface or to the direction of the playing surface, and has not yet touched your playing surface and not passed over the end line.

(9) "The server" means the player who should first hit the ball in a rally.

（10）接发球员：在一个回合中，第二个击球的运动员。

（11）裁判员：被指定管理一场比赛的人。

（12）副裁判员：被指定在某些方面协助裁判员工作的人。

（13）"穿或戴"的物品：指运动员在一个回合开始时穿或戴的任何物品，但不包括比赛用球。

（14）越过或绕过球网装置：除从球网和比赛台面之间通过以及从球网和网架之间通过的情况外，均应视为已"超过或绕过"球网装置。

（15）球台的"端线"：包括球台端线以及端线两端的无限延长线。

2. 合法发球和合法还击

（1）合法发球。

①发球时，球应放在不执拍手的手掌上，手掌张开和伸平。球应是静止的，处在发球方的端线之后和比赛台面的水平面之上。

②发球员须用手把球几乎垂直地向上抛起，不得使球旋转，并使球在离开不执拍手的手掌之后上升不少于

(10) "The receiver" means the player who should second hit the ball in a rally.

(11) "The umpire" means the person who is assigned to control a match.

(12) "The assistant umpire" means the person who is assigned to help the umpire work in some aspects.

(13) "The wearing items" mean anything a player wears at the beginning of the first rally, but they do not include the ball used for the game.

(14) "Passing over or around the net assembly" means that any ball coming from the opponent to your playing surface will be regarded as passing over or around the net assembly, except that it passes between the net and the playing surface or between the net and the net post.

(15) "The end line" which includes the end line of the table and lines of infinite extension in both ends.

2. A good service and a good return

(1) A good service.

①When serving, the ball should be put on the palm of the free hand with the palm stretched flatly. And the ball should be stationary and behind the end line of the serving side above the level of the playing surface.

②The server must almost vertically throw up the ball with the hand, which cannot make it spin. The ball should rise not less than 16 cm after leaving the palm of the free hand. And the ball cannot touch any object before

16厘米，球下降到被击出前不能碰到任何物体。

③当球从抛起的最高点下降时，发球员方可击球，使球首先触及本方台区，然后越过或绕过球网装置，再触及接发球员的台区。在双打中，球应先后触及发球员和接发球员的右半区。

④从抛球前球静止的最后一瞬间到击球时，球和球拍应在比赛台面的水平面之上。击球时，球应在发球方的端线之后，但不得超过发球员身体（手臂、头或腿除外）离端线最远的部分。

⑤运动员发球时，有责任让裁判员或副裁判员看清他是否按照合法发球的规定发球。

当裁判员怀疑发球员某个发球动作的正确性，并且他或者副裁判员都不能确定该发球动作不合法时，如果此现象是本场比赛第一次出现，裁判员可以警告发球员而不予以判分。

在同一场比赛中，如果运动员发球动作的正确性再次受到怀疑，不管是否出于同样的原因，均判接发球方得一分。

being hit out.

③ Only when the ball is descending from peak can the server hit the ball making the ball touch his(her) own court first, then pass over or around the net assembly and touch the receiver's court. In doubles the ball should first touch the right half court of the server and the receiver successively.

④ The ball and the racket should be above the level of the playing surface from the last moment, in which the ball is stationary, before being thrown up till it is struck. When hitting the ball, the ball should be behind the end line of the serving side, but not exceed the part of the server's body which is the farthest from the end line (except the head, arms or legs).

⑤ When serving, the player has the responsibility to let the umpire or the assistant umpire to see if his(her) serve is in accordance with the rules for a good service.

If the umpire doubts the correctness for any movement of the player's serve, and both he(her) or the assistant umpire cannot determine that the service is not legal, he(her) can, on the first occasion in a match, declare no score and a let; meanwhile warn the server.

If the correctness of the player's serve is doubted again in the same match, whether or not it is for the same reason, it will be determined as one point to the receiver.

无论是否是第一次，任何时候，只要发球员明显没有按照合法发球的规定发球，就将被判失一分，无需警告。

运动员因身体伤病而不能严格遵守合法发球的某些规定时，可由裁判员做出免予执行的决定，但须在赛前向裁判员说明。

（2）合法还击。

对方发球或还击后，本方运动员必须击球，使球直接越过或绕过球网装置，或触及球网装置后，再触及对方台区。

3. 比赛次序

（1）在单打中，首先由发球员合法发球，再由接发球员合法还击，然后两者交替合法还击。

（2）在双打中，首先由发球员合法发球，再由接发球员合法还击，然后由发球员的同伴合法还击，再由接发球员的同伴合法还击。此后，运动员按此次序轮流合法还击。

4. 重发球和一分

（1）重发球。

出现下列情况应判重发球：

Whether or not it is the first time or at any time, as long as the player's serve is obviously not in accordance with the rules for a good service, he(she) will be determined as loss of a point without warning.

When the player can not strictly comply with certain rules for a good service due to physical injuries, he(she) can be exempted from execution by the umpire; but he(she) must tell the umpire before the game.

(2) A good return.

After the serve or return of the opponent you must hit the ball making it directly pass over or around the net assembly, or touch the net assembly and then contact the opponent's playing surface.

3. The order of the game

(1) In singles, the server should first make a good service, then the receiver gives a good return; afterwards both players legally return in turn.

(2) In doubles, the server should first make a good service, next the receiver gives a good return, and then the server's partner returns legally; and next the receiver's partner gives a good return. Afterwards, players should make good returns in turn in that order.

4. A let and a point

(1) A let (let service).

A rally should be determined as a let in the following circumstances:

①如果发球员发出的球，在越过或绕过球网装置时、触及球网装置，此后成为合法发球或者被接发球员或其同伴阻挡。

②如果接发球员或接发球方未准备好，球已发出，接发球方没有企图击球。

③由于发生了运动员无法控制的干扰，而使运动员未能合法发球、合法还击或遵守规则。

④裁判员或副裁判员暂停比赛。

⑤在双打时，运动员错发、错接。

可以在下列情况下暂停比赛：

①由于要纠正发球、接发球次序或方位错误。

②由于要实行轮换发球法。

③由于警告或处罚运动员。

④由于比赛环境受到干扰，以致该回合结果有可能受到影响。

（2）一分。

除被判重发球的回合，下列情况下运动员得一分：

①When the ball served by the server passing over or around the net assembly, it first hits the net assembly then becomes a good service or is obstructed by the receiver or his partner.

②When the receiver or the receiving side has not got ready, the ball has been served, and the receiving side does not attempt to hit the ball.

③The player fails to do a good service, a good return or complies with the rules because an interference happens which he(she) can't control.

④The game is suspended by the umpire or the assistant umpire.

⑤In doubles, players make a mistake in the order of serve or return.

A game can be suspended in the following circumstances:

①The umpire will correct a mistake in the order of the serve, return or ends.

②The umpire will implement the expedite system.

③The umpire will warn or penalize a player.

④The game environment is disturbed, which may affect the result of the rally.

(2) A point.

Except that the rally is determined as a let, a player will score a point in the following circumstances:

①对方运动员未能合法发球或合法还击。

②运动员在发球或还击后，对方运动员在击球前，球触及除球网装置以外的任何东西。

③对方击球后，该球越过本方端线而没触及本方台区。

④对方阻挡或连击。

⑤对方用不符合规定的拍面击球。

⑥对方运动员或其穿戴的任何东西触及球网装置或使球台移动。

⑦对方运动员不执拍手触及比赛台面。

⑧双打时，对方运动员击球次序错误。

⑨执行轮换发球法时，接发球运动员或其双打同伴，包括接发球一击，完成了13次合法还击。

5. 一局比赛和一场比赛

（1）在一局比赛中，先得11分的一方为胜方。10平后，先多得2分的一方为胜方。

（2）一场比赛由奇数局组成，应采用七局四胜制或五局

① Your opponent fails to make a good service or a good return.

② After the player making a service or a return, the ball has touched anything except the net assembly before the opponent hits it.

③ After being struck by the opponent, the ball passes beyond the end line of this player without touching his (her) playing surface.

④ The opponent obstructs the ball or makes a double hit.

⑤ The opponent hits the ball with the racket face which is not in conformity with the provisions.

⑥ The opponent or anything he(she) wears and carries contacts the net assembly or moves the table.

⑦ The free hand of the opponent touches the playing surface.

⑧ In doubles, the opponents make a mistake in the order of hitting the ball.

⑨ When the expedite system is implemented, the receiver or his(her) doubles partner has completed 13 good returns including the return of service.

5. A game and a match.

(1) In a game, any side which first scores 11 points is the winner. And after the deuce of 10∶10 points, the side which will first gain a lead of 2 points is the winner.

(2) A match consists of games of odd number; and the best-four-of-seven or best-three-of-five systems should be adopted.

三胜制。一场比赛应连续进行。但在局与局之间,任何一名运动员都有权要求获得不超过1分钟的休息时间。

6. 发球、接发球和方位的选择

(1)选择发球、接发球和方位的权力应抽签来决定。中签者可以选择先发球或先接发球,或选择先在某一侧场地。

(2)当一方运动员选择了先发球或先接发球,或选择了先在某一方后,另一方运动员应有另一个选择的权力。

(3)当一方运动员2次发球之后,接发球方即成为发球方。依此类推,直至该局比赛结束,或者直至双方比分都达到10分或实行轮换发球法。这时,发球和接发球次序仍然不变,但每人只轮发一分球。

(4)在双打的第一局比赛中,先发球方确定第一发球员,再由先接发球方确定第一接发球员。在以后的各局比赛中,第一发球员确定后,第一接发球员应是前一局发球给他(她)的运动员。

(5)在双打中,每次换发球时,前面的接发球员应成为

A match should proceed continuously; but in the time between games any player has the right to request for a break which is no more than 1 min.

6. The selection of serving, receiving and ends

(1) The right to choose serving, receiving and ends should be determined by lot. The winner of the lot can choose the first serving or first receiving, or select the first end.

(2) When the player of one side has selected the first serving or first receiving, or selected the first end, the player of the other side should have the other right to choose.

(3) After the player of one side has served twice, the receiving side will become the serving side; and the rest may be deduced by analogy until the end of the game or both the sides score 10 points, or the expedite system is implemented. At this time, the order of serving and receiving remains unchanged, but each player will only serve for one point in turn.

(4) In the first game of doubles, the first serving side chooses the first server; and then receiving side chooses the first receiver. In the subsequent games, when the first server is determined, the first receiver should be the player who served to him(her) in the previous game.

(5) In doubles, every time when alternating service, the receiver in the previous game should become the server and the partner

发球员，前面的发球员的同伴应成为接发球员。

（6）一局中首先发球的一方，在该场下一局应首先接发球。在双打决胜局中，当一方先得5分时，接发球应交换接发球次序。

（7）一局中，在某一方位比赛的一方，在该场下一局应换到另一方位。在决胜局中，一方先得5分时，双方应交换方位。

7. 发球、接发球次序和方位的错误

（1）裁判员一旦发现发球、接发球次序错误，应立即暂停比赛，并根据该场比赛开始时确立的次序，按场上比分由应该发球或接发球的运动员发球或接发球；在双打中，则按发现错误时那一局中首先有发球权的一方所确立的次序进行纠正后，继续比赛。

（2）裁判员一旦发现运动员应交换方位而未交换时，应立即暂停比赛，并根据该场比赛开始时确立的次序、按场上运动员应站的正确方位进行纠正，再继续比赛。

of the server in the previous game should become the receiver.

(6) In a game, the first serving side should receive first in the next game of the match. In the deciding game of doubles, when one side first scores 5 points, the order of receiving should be exchanged for serve receiving.

(7) In a game, one side of the game in a certain end should be changed to the other end in the next game of the match. In the deciding game, when one side first scores 5 points, both the sides should exchange ends.

7. The errors in the order of serving, receiving and ends

(1) Once the umpire has found an error in the order of serving and receiving, he(she) should immediately suspend the game and get the player who should serve to serve, and the player who should receive to receive, according to the order established at the beginning of the match and the scores in play. In doubles, an error in the order of serving and receiving should be corrected according to the order established by the side, which has the right to serve first in the game in which the error is detected. After the correction the match should be kept on.

(2) Once the umpire has found that the players should have exchange ends, but they have not done so, he should immediately suspend the game and correct it according to the order established at the beginning of the match and the correct ends the players should stand. And then the match should be kept on.

（3）无论何时，发现错误之前的所有得分均有效。

8. 轮换发球法

（1）如果一局比赛进行到10分钟仍未结束（双方都已获得至少9分除外），或者在此之前任何时间，应双方运动员要求，应实行轮换发球法。

①当时限到时，球仍处于比赛状态，裁判员应立即暂停比赛。以后由被暂停回合的发球员发球，继续比赛。

②当时限到时，球未处于比赛状态，应由前一回合的接球员发球，继续比赛。

（2）此后，每个运动员都轮发一分球，直至该局结束。如果接发球方进行了13次合法还击，则判发球方失一分。

（3）轮换发球法一经实行，或一局比赛进行了10分钟，该场比赛剩余的各局都必须实行轮换发球法。

第二节
乒乓球裁判法简介

1. 裁判员的职责

裁判工作是乒乓球运动的重要组成部分。每场比赛

(3) In any circumstance, all the points scored before the discovery of an error are valid.

8. The expedite system

(1) If a game is still not over after 10-minute play (except that both sides have scored at least 9 points) or at any earlier time before at the request of players of both sides, the expedite system should be implemented.

① If the ball is still in play when the time limit is reached, the umpire should immediately suspend the game, afterwards, get the player who was the server in the suspended rally to serve, and go on the match.

② If the ball is not in play, when the time limit is reached, the umpire should get the player who was the receiver in the previous rally to serve, and go on the match.

(2) Hereafter, each player will only serve for one point alternately until the end of the game. If the receiving side has made 13 good returns, the serving side will be determined as loss of a point.

(3) Once the expedite system is implemented or a game has proceeded for 10 min, the following games of the match must implement the expedite system.

Section 2
Brief introduction to the referee law of table tennis

1. The duties of an umpire

The refereeing work is an important part of table tennis. One umpire and one assistant

均应指派1名裁判员和1名副裁判员。裁判员应对下列事项负责：

（1）检查运动员的球拍、服装是否符合规则。

（2）主持抽签确定发球、接发球和方位。

（3）保证方位和发球、接发球的次序的正确。

（4）决定每一个回合得1分或重发球。

（5）根据规定的程序报分。

（6）保持比赛的连续性。（只允许运动员每6分球擦一次汗）

2. 副裁判员的职责

（1）决定处于比赛状态中的球是否触及距离他（她）最近的边线的上边缘。

（2）有违反场外指导行为规定时，通知裁判员。

3. 裁判员和副裁判员的共同职责

（1）能够判定运动员发球动作是否合法。

（2）能够判定合法发球在

umpire should be assigned to each match. The umpire should be in charge of the following proceedings:

(1) The umpire should check whether or not the rackets and clothing of players conform to the provisions of the rules.

(2) The umpire should preside over the draw to determine the server, receiver and ends.

(3) The umpire should ensure ends and the order of the serving and receiving to be correct.

(4) The umpire should determine whether 1 point is scored or a let service is given in each rally.

(5) The umpire should announce scores according to the regulated procedures.

(6) The umpire should maintain the continuity of the game. (Players should be only allowed to wipe away sweat once every six points.)

2. The duties of an assistant umpire

(1) The assistant umpire should determine whether or not the ball in play touches the upper edge of the sideline which is nearest to him(her).

(2) The assistant umpire should notify the umpire when the provisions for the bench coaching or behaviors are violated.

3. The common duty of an umpire and an assistant umpire

(1) They both can determine whether or not a service action of a player is illegal.

(2) They both can determine whether or not

球越过或绕过球网装置时是否触及球网装置。

（3）能够判定运动员是否阻挡。

（4）能够判定比赛环境是否受到意外干扰，该回合的结果是否受到影响。

（5）能够掌握练习时间、比赛时间及间歇时间。

4. 裁判手势

手势是裁判员在执行规则时的动作。

比赛中，裁判员为了向运动员和观众说明得分、失误的原因，使他们及时了解比赛的进行情况；特别是国际比赛，由于语言不通，或因比赛场内球台多、人声嘈杂，就更需要采用手势和术语来表达。手势和术语，要精练、明确、果断，动作要大方。明显现象可以不必用术语和手势。

（1）在比赛开始时，允许运动员先有两分钟的练习时间。（如图6-1）

（2）当练习时间到要停止练习，或判发球擦网、发球犯规、暂停、时间到、台面移动、连击、两跳、重发球和中断比

the ball in a good service contacts the net assembly when passing over or around it.

(3) They both can determine whether or not a player obstructs the ball.

(4) They both can determine whether or not the result of the rally may be affected when the game environment is disturbed by accident.

(5) They both can control the time for the practice, game and intervals.

4. The refereeing gestures

The refereeing gestures are the actions of an umpire in the execution of the rules.

In a game, the umpire needs to use the gestures and terms in order to explain the cause of scoring and fault to players and spectators, making them know the situations in the game timely. And the gestures and terms are more needed for the expression especially in the international competitions, due to the language barrier or more tables in the match court with a hubbub of voices. So, the gestures and terms should be concise, clear and decisive; and the actions should be decent. When the phenomena are obvious, the gestures and terms should not be necessarily used.

(1) At the beginning of a game, players are allowed to practice first for two minutes; and the umpire should gesture with the right hand. (As shown in fig. 6-1)

(2) The umpire should raise the right hand and shout out terms at the same time in the following cases: the practice time is up and the practice should be stopped. Or a serve is determined as net. A serve is faulted. A

赛时，裁判员应将右手高举，同时喊出术语。（如图6-2）

game should be suspended; or time is up. The playing surface is moved; or the ball is determined as double hit, double bounce; and a serve is determined as a let. (As shown in fig. 6-2)

图 6-1　练习两分钟
Fig. 6-1　Practice for two minutes

图 6-2　停止练习、时间到、暂停、发球擦网、发球犯规、台面移动、连击、两跳、重发球
Fig. 6-2　Stop practice, Time's up, Suspension, Net service, Service fault, Moved playing surface, Double hit, Double bounce, Let service

（3）当判得分时，裁判员应将靠近得分方的手臂举起。（如图6-3）

(3) When a point scored is determined, the umpire should raise the arm which is close to the scoring side. (As shown in fig. 6-3)

图 6-3 得分
Fig. 6-3 Scoring

（4）当判擦边时，裁判员应用食指指向擦边处。（如图 6-4）

(4) When an edge ball is determined, the umpire should point to the sideswipe location with the forefinger. (As shown in fig. 6-4)

图 6-4 擦边球
Fig. 6-4 Edge ball

（5）当一局比赛开始或交换发球时，应指向下一个即将发球者（该手势同样适用于一局比赛或一场比赛结束后，裁判员宣布比赛结果时，手臂指向获胜方）。（如图 6-5）

(5) When a game starts or the players change service, the umpire should point to the next server (after a game or a match is over when announcing the result of the match, the umpire should equally use the gesture to point to the winning side). (As shown in fig. 6-5)

图 6-5 交换发球时指向下一个即将发球者
Fig. 6-5 When exchanging service, the umpire should point to the next server.

（6）当判阻挡时，裁判员应示意阻挡手势，同时喊出术语。（如图 6-6）

(6) When an obstruction is determined, the umpire should give the gesture for obstruction and shout out the term at the same time. (As shown in fig. 6-6)

（7）当一局比赛结束后，或者决胜局任何一方达到第 5 分时，需要运动员交换场地，裁判员应用手势示意，同时喊出术语。（如图 6-7）

(7) When a game is over or any side scores to 5 points in the deciding game, the players need to change ends, the umpire should give the gesture and shout out the term at the same time. (As shown in fig. 6-7)

图 6-6 阻挡
Fig. 6-6 Obstruct

图 6-7 交换方位
Fig. 6-7 Change ends

（8）当一局比赛开始时，裁判员应示意接球方和发球方。（如图6-8）

(8) At the beginning of a game, the umpire should give the gesture to show the receiving side and serving side. (As shown in fig. 6-8)

图 6–8　准备、发球
Fig. 6–8　Ready and serve

在临场执法时，主裁判需上身端坐，两腿及双膝尽量靠拢，双手自然放在双膝或座椅扶手或裁判椅搭板上。在比赛过程中，主裁判应身体略微前倾，全神贯注地关注比赛。

In the on-site law enforcement, the umpire should sit up decently with the upper body upright and the two legs and knees drawn as close as possible; meanwhile, put both hands naturally on the knees or the armrests of the umpire's chair. In the process of the game, the umpire should lean forward slightly keeping a watchful eye on the match.

第三节
乒乓球比赛及类型简介

Section 3
Brief introduction to the table tennis match and its types

1. 世界乒乓球锦标赛

世界乒乓球锦标赛简称"世乒赛"，它是国际乒乓球联合会主办的一项最高水平的世界乒乓球大赛，每届比赛由国际乒乓球联合会授权比赛

1. World Table Tennis Championships

World Table Tennis Championships is abbreviated as WTTC, which is a world table tennis competition of the highest level hosted by the International Table Tennis Federation. For each session of the game, the International Table Tennis Federation will authorize the

地乒乓球协会主办，具有广泛的影响力。

首届世乒赛于 1926 年 12 月在英国伦敦举行，从 1959 年第 25 届开始改为每两年举办一次。世乒赛与乒乓球世界杯、奥运会乒乓球比赛并称为"乒乓球运动的三大赛事"。

自 2003 年第 47 届世乒赛起，单项比赛于奇数年举行，团体赛于偶数年举行，到目前已经举办了 54 届世乒赛（截至 2018 年）。

世界乒乓球锦标赛包括 7 个项目：男子团体、女子团体、男子单打、女子单打、男子双打、女子双打和混合双打。每个项目设有一个奖杯：

男子团体——斯韦思林杯
女子团体——考比伦杯
男子单打——圣·勃莱德杯
女子单打——吉·盖斯特杯
男子双打——伊朗杯
女子双打——波普杯
混合双打——兹·赫杜塞克杯

世界乒乓球男子团体锦标赛（斯韦思林杯）的比赛规则：

（1）各单位可报 5 名选手参加比赛，每次比赛双方可以从中挑选 3 名选手出场，每名

table tennis association of the host place to sponsor the game; and it has a wide influence.

The first session was held in December 1926 in London, England. It has been changed to be held once every two years since the 25th session in 1959. World Table Tennis Championships, World Cup Table Tennis and Olympic Table Tennis are called as "the three major events in table tennis".

Since the 47th world championships of 2003 it has been changed to hold the competition of individual events in odd-numbered years and the team events in even-numbered years. So far 54 sessions of World Table Tennis Championships have been held (As of 2018).

World Table Tennis Championships includes seven events: men's team, women's team, men's singles, women's singles, men's doubles, women's doubles and mixed doubles. Each event has a trophy:

Men's team	Swaythling Cup
Women's team	M Corbillon Cup
Men's singles	St. Bride Vase
Women's singles	G.Geist Prize
Men's doubles	Iran Cup
Women's doubles	Pope Trophy
Mixed doubles	Zdenek Haydusek Prize

The contesting rules for the men's team event of World Table Tennis Championships (Swaythling Cup) is like the followings.

(1) Each unit can sign up 5 players to take part in the competition. Both sides can choose 3 players from among the 5 players to play in each match; and each player can

运动员出场 2 次。

（2）比赛采用 5 场 3 胜制（每场比赛亦采用 5 局 3 胜制）。1、2、4、5 场为单打，第 3 场为双打。在打完前两场比赛后再确定双打运动员的出场名单。

（3）比赛前，双方用抽签的方法选定主、客队。主队 3 名选手定为 A、B、C；客队 3 名选手定为 X、Y、Z。

（4）比赛顺序如下：

(2) The best of five games is adopted in the competition (the best of five games is also used for each match). The 1st, 2nd, 4th and 5th games are for singles; and the 3rd game is for doubles. The roster of the players for the doubles should be determined after the first two games are finished.

(3) Before the match the two sides should draw by lot to select the host team and the guest team. The 3 players of the host team should be set as A, B, C; and the 3 players of the guest team should be set as X, Y, Z.

(4) The order of competition is like the followings.

	主队	客队
第一场	A	X
第二场	B	Y
第三场	C+A 或 B	Z+X 或 Y
第四场	A 或 B	Z
第五场	C	X 或 Y

	The host team	The guest team
The 1st match session	A	X
The 2nd match session	B	Y
The 3rd match session	C+A or B	Z+X or Y
The 4th match session	A or B	Z
The 5th match session	C	X or Y

世界乒乓球女子团体锦标赛（考比伦杯）的比赛规则。

（1）各单位可报 4 名选手参加比赛，每次比赛双方可以从中挑选 2 名选手参加单打，再从 4 名选手中任选 2 名选手配对参加排在第 3 场的双打。

The contesting rules for the women's team event of World Table Tennis Championships (M Corbillon Cup) is like the followings.

(1) Each unit can sign up 4 players to take part in the competition. Both sides can select 2 players from among the 4 players to play in singles and then willfully choose 2 players from among the 4 players to pair for the doubles in the 3rd game.

（2）比赛采用5场3胜制（每场比赛亦采用5局3胜制），以先赢得3场者为胜方。

（3）比赛前，双方用抽签的方法选定主、客队。主队2名单打选手定为A、B；客队2名单打选手定为X、Y。

（4）5场比赛的次序为：

(2) The best of five games is adopted in the competition (the best of five games is also used for each match). Any side which first wins three games is the winner.

(3) Before the match the two sides should draw by lot to select the host team and the guest team. The 2 players of the host team who will play the singles game, should be set as A, B; and the 2 players of the guest team who will play the singles game, should be set as X, Y.

(4) The order of the 5 games is like the followings.

	主队	客队
第一场	A	X
第二场	B	Y
第三场	C+A 或 B	Z+X 或 Y
第四场	A 或 B	Z
第五场	C	X 或 Y

	The host team	The guest team
The 1st match session	A	X
The 2nd match session	B	Y
The 3rd match session	C+A or B	Z+X or Y
The 4th match session	A or B	Z
The 5th match session	C	X or Y

2. 世界杯赛

为了进一步推动世界乒乓球运动的发展，国际乒联于1980年8月举办了首届世界杯男子单打比赛，由国际乒联公布的最新世界排名在前6名的选手和上届冠军、六大洲的单打冠军或代表、主办协会的1名选手，以及国际乒联推荐的2名运动员

2. Table Tennis World Cup

In order to further promote the development of the world table tennis, International Table Tennis Federation held the first World Cup men's singles match in August 1980. A total of 16 competitors was made up by the first six players in the latest world rankings released by the international table tennis federation, the defending champion, the singles titles or the representatives from the six continents and one player of the organizing association, as well as two players recommended by International

共16名选手组成参赛选手。此后每年举行一届。1990年增设了团体赛和双打比赛，1996年9月增设了女子单打比赛。

3. 奥运会乒乓球比赛

由国际乒联申请，1981年在巴登召开的第84届国际奥委会会议上，决定将乒乓球列入1988年奥运会正式比赛项目。比赛由64名男选手和32名女选手角逐男子单打、女子单打、男子双打和女子双打4项冠军。

2008年北京奥运会，由男子团体和女子团体替代男子双打和女子双打。比赛共四个项目：男子团体、女子团体、男子单打、女子单打。团体赛每队由3名运动员出场，其比赛方式为：

Table Tennis Federation. Since then it has been held once a year. The team and doubles competitions were added in 1990; and the women's singles match was established in September 1996.

3. The Olympic table tennis competition

For the application by International Table Tennis Federation, at the 84th session of the International Olympic Committee meeting held in Baden, table tennis was decided to be an official event in the 1988 Olympic Games. In the game 64 male players and 32 female players compete for champions in 4 events of men's singles, women's singles, men's doubles and women's doubles.

Since 2008 Beijing Olympic Games it has been changed to replace men's doubles and women's doubles with men's team and women's team events. There are a total of four events in the competition: men's team and women's team, men's singles and women's singles. In the team events each team will play by three players, and its contesting rules are as follows:

	主队	客队
第一场	A	X
第二场	B	Y
第三场	C+A 或 B	Z+X 或 Y
第四场	A 或 B	Z
第五场	C	X 或 Y

	The host team	The guest team
The 1st match session	A	X
The 2nd match session	B	Y
The 3rd match session	C+A or B	Z+X or Y
The 4th match session	A or B	Z
The 5th match session	C	X or Y

第四节
乒乓球运动竞赛方法

目前，乒乓球运动竞赛的基本方法常用的有单循环赛和单淘汰赛两种。

1. 单循环赛

单循环赛，就是参加比赛的队（或运动员）之间轮流比赛一次。这种比赛办法能使参加比赛的各队（或运动员）之间都有比赛的机会，有利于通过比赛全面地进行经验交流。比赛结果的偶然性机遇性小，因而能较准确地反映出参加比赛的各队（或运动员）的真正水平和名次。但循环赛场次多，比赛时间长，名次的确定又易受其他队的影响。因此，循环赛的队数（人数）不宜过多。参加队（或人数）过多时，可采用分组循环赛的办法来进行。

（1）单循环赛轮数和场次的计算：在单循环赛中各队（或运动员）普遍出场比赛一

Section 4
Competition methods of table tennis

At present, there are two kinds of the basic rules in common use for table tennis competitions, which are the round robin tournament and the single elimination tournament.

1. The round robin tournament

The round robin tournament (or all-play-all tournament) is a competition in which each team (or player) meets all other teams (or players) once in turn. This contesting rules can make all the teams (or players) in the competition have a chance to play with one another and help them fully exchange experience through the game. With less contingency and chance causes in the result of the match, thus it can accurately reflect the real levels and rankings of the teams (or player) in the competition. But the round robin tournament needs more game sessions and a long playing time; and in the meantime, the determination of rankings is easily influenced by other teams. Therefore, the participating teams (or players) in the round robin tournament should not be excessive. If there are too many participating teams (or players) in the round robin tournament, the group round robin can be adopted to play the game.

(1) The count for the numbers of rounds and game sessions in the round robin tournament: that all the teams (or players) in the round robin tournament play one time

次（包含轮空），称为"一轮"。每两个队之间比赛一次，称为"一次比赛"；每两个人（两对）之间比赛一次，称为"一场比赛"。

①轮数的计算：

参加比赛的队（或人）数是奇数时：轮数 = 队数（或人数）；参加比赛的队（或人）数是偶数时：轮数 = 队数（或人数）−1。

②场数的计算：场数 = n（n−1）/2 其中 n 为参加的队（或人）数。

（2）单循环赛比赛顺序的确定：确定单循环比赛顺序的方法很多。而乒乓球比赛通常采用的方法是"1号位固定，逆时针轮转法"。示例：6个队参加比赛的排法

(including a bye) is called as "a round". A competition between every two teams is called as "a team match"; and a contest between every two players (or pairs) is called as "a game match".

① The count for the number of rounds :

When the number of the teams (or players) competing in a contest is an odd number: the number of rounds = the number of the teams (or players).When the number of the teams (or players) competing in a contest is an even number: the number of rounds = the number of the teams (or players)−1.

② The count for the number of game sessions: the numbers of game sessions = n (n−1)/2, in which n represents the number of the teams (or players) competing in a contest.

(2) The determination for the order of competition in the round robin tournament: there are many ways to determine the order of competition in the round robin tournament. However, the method commonly used in the table tennis game is to cycle anticlockwise with No.1 position fixed. Now, take the order for six teams in the competition for an example.

第1轮 The first round	第2轮 The second round	第3轮 The third round	第4轮 The fourth round	第5轮 The fifth round
1—6	1—5	1—4	1—3	1—2
2—5	6—4	5—3	4—2	3—6
3—4	2—3	6—2	5—6	4—5

如果是奇数队参赛，比如5个队参加循环赛，可以用一个"0"放在"6"的位置补成双数，凡与"0"相遇的队，该轮"轮空"。

If the number of teams in the competition is an odd, such as the five teams in a round robin tournament, a "0" can be used to fill in the "6" position making it into an even number. Every team which encounters with "0" will be off a bye.

根据现有的规则：如果小组预选选出一名运动员或一队，则该小组的最后一场比赛应在小组排列第一或第二位的运动员或队之间进行；如果小组预选选出两名运动员或两队，则该小组的最后一场比赛应该在小组排列第二和第三位的运动员或队之间进行，并依此类推。

在实际操作时应根据各组出线的人（队）数，适当调整比赛的轮次。如规定小组前2名出线，可把第2轮调至最后一轮进行。

（3）单循环赛名次计算：

第一步：根据所获得的场次分数决定。胜一场得2分，输一场得1分，未出场比赛或未完成比赛的场次得0分。

第二步：如果小组的两名或更多的运动员得分数相同，名次应按他们相互之间比赛的成绩决定。首先计算他们之间获得的场次分数，再根据需要计算个人比赛场次（团体赛时）、局和分的胜负比率，直至算出名次为止。

It is stipulated according to the existing rules: if one player or one team will be chosen in a preliminary group, the last match should be played between you or team that ranks first and the you or team that ranks second in the preliminary group. If two players or two teams will be chosen in a preliminary group, the last match should be played between you or team that ranks second and the you or team that ranks third in the preliminary group; and the rest may be determined by analogy.

Therefore in the actual operation, the number of rounds in the tournament should be properly adjusted according to the number of players (teams) qualified for the next round in each group. For example, if the regulation stipulates that the players ranking first two in a preliminary group should be qualified for the next round, then the second round can be adjusted to the last round to play.

(3) The count of ranking in the round robin tournament:

The first step: it is determined according to the obtained scores of match sessions. Winning a match session will gain 2 scores; and losing a match session will gain 1 score. The match session which is unfinished or not played will gain no scores.

The second step: if two or more players in a group have gained the same scores, the ranks should be determined on the basis of the game results one another among them. First, you should count the obtained scores of match sessions among them, and then as needed you should count the ratios of winning or losing in individual match sessions (in team events), games and scores until work out the rankings.

第三步：如果在任何阶段已经决定出一个或更多成员的名次后，其他小组成员仍然得分相同，为决定相同分数成员的名次，再根据第一步和第二步的程序继续计算时，应将已决定出名次的成员的比赛成绩删除。

如果按照以上各步的程序仍不能决定某些队（人）的名次时，这些队（人）的名次将由抽签来决定。

The third step: if at any stages, after the rankings of one or more players (or teams) have been determined, the other players (or teams) in the group still have the same scores, in order to determine the rankings of the players (or teams) who have the same scores, you should go on the count. But when you continue to count according to the first and the second steps, you should delete the competition results of the players (or teams) whose rankings have been determined.

If the rankings of some teams (or players) still cannot be determined in accordance with the various steps above, the rankings of these teams (or players) will be determined by drawing lots.

乒乓球团体赛成绩示例
A sample for scores of a table tennis team match

	A	B	C	D	E	F	G	得分 scores	计算 count	名次 ranking
A		3:1	2:3	2:3	3:1	0:3	3:1	9	4,3,1/1,5/4	4
B	1:3		2:3	3:0	3:2	1:3	3:1	9	4,3,1/1,4/3	3
C	3:2	3:2		3:2	L	0:3	3:2	9	6	2
D	3:2	0:3	2:3		3:0	2:3	3:2	9	4,3,1/1,3/5	5
E	1:3	2:3	3:0	0:3		1:3	2:3	7	1	7
F	3:0	3:1	3:0	3:2	3:1		3:0	12		1
G	1:3	1:3	1:3	2:3	3:2	0:3		7	2	6

（4）名次计算过程说明：

①通过第一步的计算，得分最高的是得12分，F获得了第一名。

② 得分其次的是A、B、C、D，它们同得9分，将获得第二名 至第五名，先计算它们彼此之间的得分，A、B、

(4) The description of the counting process for ranking:

① Through the count of the first step, team F gains the highest score of 12 points which ranks the first.

② Team A, team B, team C and team D are the second in scoring, they all scores 9 points and will get the second to the fifth. We should first count the scores between one another among them. We've found team

D 分别得 4 分，C 得 6 分，因此 C 为第二名；再计算 A、B、D 彼此之间的得分，它们的得分相同，均为 3 分，此时要计算这三队之间的胜负比率（胜 / 负），按 "次、场、局、分" 顺序进行计算：次率计算：A 为 1/1，B 为 1/1，D 为 1/1；

场率计算：A 为 5/4=1.25，B 为 4/3=1.33，D 为 3/5=0.6；因此 B 获第三名，A 获第四名，D 获第五名。

③同理，E 与 G 同得 7 分，它们将分别获得第六名和第七名，计算这两队之间的得分，G 胜 E 得 2 分，E 得 1 分，因此，G 为第六名，E 为第七名。

2. 单淘汰赛

单淘汰赛是将所有参加比赛的运动员（队）编排成一定的比赛次序，由相邻的两名运动员（队）进行比赛，负方淘汰，胜方进入下一轮，直到剩下最后一名运动员（队），这名运动员（队）就是单淘汰赛的冠军。

A, team B and team D have gotten 4 points respectively and team C has gained 6 points, therefore team C is the second. And then we should count the scores between one another among team A, team B and team D; subsequently, we've found they all have gotten the same score of 3 points. By this time, we should count the ratios of winning or losing (win/ loss) among the three teams and do the count according to the sequence of matches, match sessions, games, and scores. Counting the ratios of matches: team A is 1/1; team B is 1/1; and team D is 1/1.

Counting the ratios of match sessions: team A is 5/4=1.25; team B is 4/3=1.33; and team D is 3/5 = 0.6. Therefore, team B ranks the third; team A gets the fourth; and team D gets the fifth place.

③Counting in a similar way, both team E and team G have gotten the same score of 7 points; and they will rank the sixth and seventh respectively. And now we should count the scores between the two teams. Team G defeats team E scoring 2 points, and team E scores 1 point. Therefore, team G gets the sixth place and team E is the seventh.

2. The single elimination tournament

The single elimination tournament is that all the players (or teams) which take part in the game will be arranged into a certain order of competition; and the two neighboring players (or teams) will have a match, afterwards the loser will be eliminated and the winner can enter into the next round until the last player (or team) will be remained. The player (or team) will be the champion of the single elimination tournament.

单淘汰赛制适合参赛的运动员（队）多、时间短、场地较少的比赛。其对抗性强，可使比赛逐步形成高潮；但因比赛场次少，互相学习和锻炼的机会也少，而最后排定名次的合理性差，机遇性强，故比赛的最后结果不一定能确切反映出运动员（或队）的综合能力。因此，在采用单淘汰赛的办法时必须采取一系列措施，尽量减少它的偶然性，力求使比赛合理、公正。

（1）单淘汰赛轮数和场数的计算。

① 轮数的计算：单淘汰赛所选用的号码位置数（2的乘方）的指数即为轮数。2的几次方即为几轮。例如：16个号码位置，$2^4=16$，即为4轮；32个号码位置，$2^5=32$，即为5轮。

② 场数的计算：场数＝人数－1。例如64人参加单淘汰赛，比赛场数为64－1＝63场。

（2）单淘汰赛比赛秩序的确定。

The method of the single elimination tournament is suitable for the tournament in which too many players (or teams) participate with a short period of time and less competition venues. Its rivalry is strong, which can make the competition gradually create high tide. But due to less game sessions, players have fewer opportunities to exercise and learn from each other. Moreover, the ranking scheduled in the end may not be quite reasonable and has some causes of chance. So, the final result of the tournament can not exactly reflect the comprehensive ability of players (or teams). And for this reason, when using the method of the single elimination tournament, a series of measures must be taken to minimize its contingency and strive to make the game reasonable and fair.

(1) The count for the numbers of rounds and game sessions in the single elimination tournament.

①The count for the numbers of rounds: The exponent of number of the number positions (the power of 2) selected in the single elimination tournament is considered to be the number of rounds. The number of power of 2 means the number of rounds. For example, 16 number positions, $2^4 = 16$, that is 4 rounds; 32 number positions, $2^5 = 32$, that is 5 rounds.

②The count for the number of game sessions: The number of game sessions = the number of players−1. For example, 64 people will participate in the single elimination tournament, the number of game sessions is 64−1 = 63 game sessions.

(2) The determination of competition order in the single elimination tournament.

① 选择号码位置数：采用单淘汰的比赛办法时，应先根据参加比赛的人数选择最接近 2 的乘方数作为号码位置数。比赛常用的号码位置数有：

2^3=8，2^4=16，2^5=32，2^6 = 64，2^7=128，2^8=256

如 16 人参加淘汰赛的比赛秩序如下：

① Selecting the number of number positions: when using the contesting rules of the single elimination, we should first select the closest power of 2 as the number of number positions according to the number of participants in the game. The numbers of number positions commonly used in competitions are as follows:

2^3=8，2^4=16，2^5=32，2^6=64，2^7=128，2^8=256

For example, the competition order in the single elimination tournament of 16 participants is shown as below:

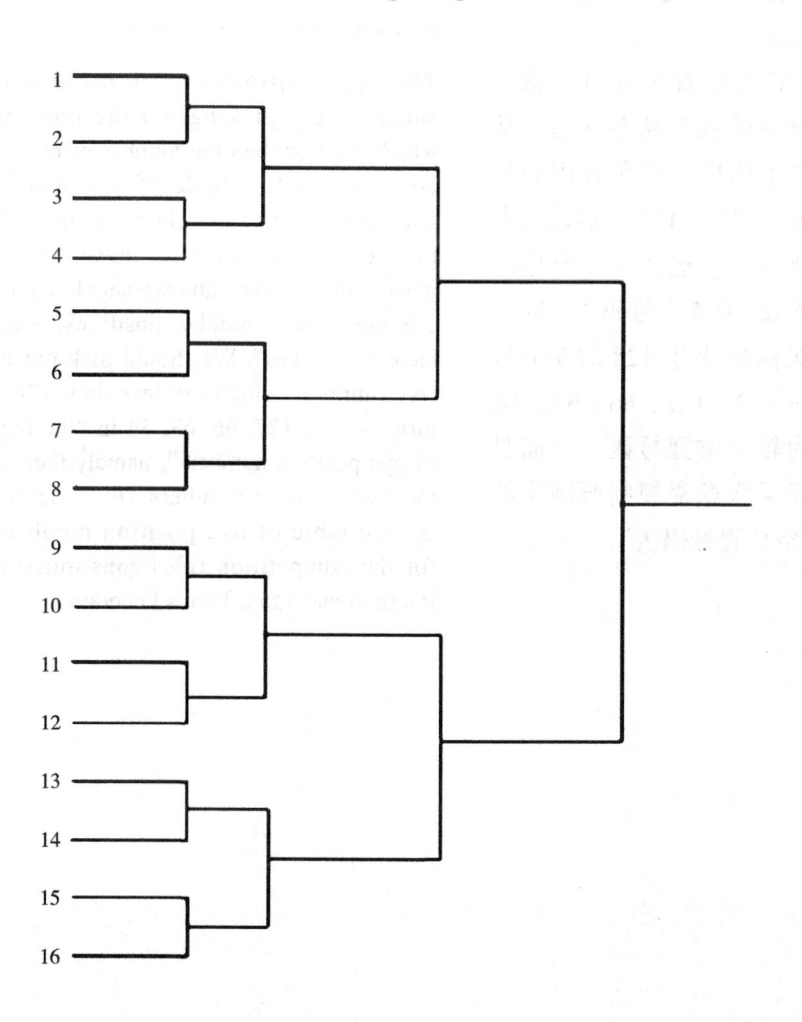

（3）轮空与抢号。

① 轮空：在单淘汰第一轮比赛中，运动员少于号码位置数时，没有运动员的位置称为"轮空"位置。轮空位置的安排，一般是种子选手先轮空（按种子选手序号顺序先后安排）。轮空的位置需按均匀分布在各区内的原则进行安排。

轮空数 = 号码位置数 – 运动员数。

轮空位置可通过《轮空位置号码表》从左往右，从上向下摘出小于所选用的号码数。例如，123名运动员参加比赛，应选用128个号码位置数，有5个号码"轮空"，依次摘出小于128的5个号码——2、127、66、63、34，即为轮空位置号码。下面是国际乒联竞赛规则所制定的"轮空位置号码表"。

(3) To have a bye and grab a number.

① A bye: in the first round competition of the single elimination tournament when the number of players is less than number of number positions, a position without a player is called as "a bye" position. For the arrangement of the bye positions, generally, the seeded players should be first arranged into the bye positions (arranged according to the serial number sequence of seeded players). The bye positions need to be distributed evenly in every region.

The number of byes=the number of number positions – the number of players.

The bye positions can be decided by successively picking out the numbers which are less than the number of number positions in "the table of bye position numbers" from left to right and from the top down. For example, there are 123 players in a contest, and we should choose 128 numbers of number positions, which have five "byes". We should pick out the five numbers which are less than 128 in turn —— 2, 127, 66, 63, 34 in "the table of bye position numbers"; namely they are the bye position numbers.The following is "the table of bye position numbers" for the competition rules constituted by International Table Tennis Federation:

轮空位置号码表
The table of bye position numbers

2	255	130	127	66	191	194	63
34	223	162	95	98	159	226	31
18	239	146	111	82	175	210	47
50	207	178	79	114	143	242	15
10	247	138	119	74	183	202	55
42	215	170	87	106	151	234	23
26	231	154	103	90	167	218	39
58	199	186	71	122	135	250	7
6	251	134	123	70	187	198	59
38	219	166	91	102	155	230	27
22	235	150	107	86	171	214	43
54	203	182	75	118	139	246	11
14	243	142	115	78	179	206	51
46	211	174	83	110	147	238	19
30	227	158	99	94	163	222	35
62	195	190	67	126	131	254	3

② 抢号：如果参加比赛的人数稍大于号码位置数时，也可采用"抢号"的方法来解决。"抢号"位置的确定和"轮空"的位置是一样的，"抢号"位置号码可用"轮空"位置表查得。例如，10名运动员参加比赛，采用单淘汰赛制，使用8个号码位置，"抢号"数2个，"抢号"位置号码查乒乓球轮空位置表得2、7。

（4）"种子"选手的确定：为了避免强队或强手在单淘汰赛的第一轮相遇而造成比

② To grab a number:If the number of participants in the game is a little more than the number of number positions, the method of "grabbing a number" can be adopted to resolve. The determination of a position for "grabbing a number" is the same with that for "a bye" position. A position number for "grabbing a number" can also be found out in "the table of bye position numbers". For example, there are 10 participants in the game with the single elimination tournament, and we use 8 number positions, which have 2 position numbers for grabbing. The position numbers for grabbing are found to be 2 and 7 in "the table of bye position numbers".

(4) The determination of the seeded teams (or players): in order to avoid the meeting among top teams or top players in the first round of the single elimination tournament

赛的不合理，可采用设立"种子"队（选手）的办法，即把一部分强队或强手确定为"种子"，均匀地分布在各个"区"内，使他们最后相遇，力求比赛结果更加合理，尽量减少偶然性。

① "种子"选手的确定："种子"是根据技术水平的高低确定的。技术水平主要是看以往的比赛成绩，一般是小比赛服从大比赛，远比赛服从近比赛。

② "种子"的数量："种子"的数量主要是根据参加比赛队数（或人数）的多少来确定。一般每6～12人（队）设一名"种子"。

causing an unreasonable competition, the method of setting up the seeded teams (or players) can be used. Namely, some top teams or top players are determined to be the seeded teams or seeded players that are evenly distributed in every region, making them meet at last, which can get a more reasonable result of the competition and minimize the contingency.

① The determination of "seeds": the "seeds" are determined based on the high and low level of techniques. The level of techniques is mainly measured according to the results of past competitions. Generally small games should submit to big games, and the past games should submit to recent games.

② The number of "seeds": the number of "seeds" is determined based on the number of teams (or players) in the game; and generally, one "seed" should be set for every 6～12 teams (or players).

附 录
Appendix

乒乓球裁判员常用术语

术语	使用环境
练习两分钟	比赛开始前，球员可以练习两分钟
停止练习	练习时间到了，应该停止练习
比赛开始，准备－发球，0:0	比赛将开始，裁判应宣布开始
犯规	比赛时，球员违反了规则
暂停，重发球	比赛被打断，或发球擦网
发球擦网	发球员发出的球，在越过或绕过球网装置时，触及球网装置，此后成为合法发球
擦边球	球被打在比赛台面的上边缘
连击	运动员用球拍和执拍手手腕以下部位连续两次击球，其间又没有触及对方比赛台面
两跳	球落在台面跳起两次。有效的回球必须是在一跳之后二跳之前完成
出界	发球或回球落在对方台面以外
阻挡	球在台面上方或正向比赛台面方向运动尚未触及本方台区、也未越过端线之前，本方运动员或其穿戴的任何物品触及到它
时间到	比赛中的休息时间或暂停时间终止
得分	任何一方在一个回合后赢得一分
暂停	一方获得合理的暂停要求
交换发球	11分制规定每人发2个球，然后交换发球权
交换方位	一局中在某一方位比赛的一方，在下一局应换到另一方位。单打决胜局中，当有一方满5分时应交换方位
不执拍手扶台	运动员在比赛进行中，不执拍手触及台面，裁判员应按相关条款判该运动员失一分
0:1；2:3	在比赛中报分
史密斯胜，11:9	
各胜一局	
第一局（第二）（第三）	
史密斯以2:1（局）领先	
史密斯以3:1获胜	
台面移动	运动员在击球过程中，身体接触台面使台子发生位置上的移动。该运动员要被判失一分
发球失误	球没过网和没有先接触自方的球台，或者接触自方球台后没有接触到对方球台。这会给对方直接加上一分
次序错误 方位错误	发现发球、接发球次序或方位错误应立即暂停，纠正后继续比赛
处罚一分	运动员在比赛中违反某些规定要被判失一分
五局三胜制	赢三局获胜
七局四胜制	赢四局获胜
再平分	运动员比分又打平
决胜局	决定胜负的一局
局点	一局中的决胜分

Common terms for table tennis umpires

Terms	Usage environment
Practice for two minutes	At the beginning of a game, the players are allowed to practice first for two minutes
Stop practice	When the practice time is up, the practice should be stopped
Begin playing, Ready-serve, Love all	A game will start, and the umpire should announce the beginning
Fault	When playing, a player breaks the rule
Let	When play is interrupted for any reason during a rally or a serve touches the net
Net	When the ball which is served by the server, passing over or around the net assembly, it first hits the net assembly then becomes a good service
Edge ball	The ball is hit on the top edge of the playing surface
Double hit	A player hits the ball twice in a row with the racket and the part below the wrist of the racket hand, during which the ball does not touch the playing surface of the opponent
Double bounce	The ball falls on the playing surface and bounces twice (An effective return must be completed after the first bounce before the second bounce)
Out	When serving or returning, the ball is hit outside the playing surface of the opponent
Obstruct	When the ball is travelling above your playing surface and has not yet touched your playing surface and not passed over the end line, you or anything you wear touch it
Time	The rest period or pause time runs out
Point	Any side wins a point after a rally
Time out	The break time or the pause time in a game is terminated
Change service	In the 11-point system, each player should serve twice, and then exchange the right to serve
Change ends	In the game you play in a certain end, in the next game you should change to the other end. In the singles decider when any side scores 5 points, the two players should exchange ends
Free hand on table	If a player's free hand touches on the table-board in the match, according to the relevant provisions the umpire should determine loss of 1 point for you
Love-one 0:1	Call the scores in the match
Two-three 2:3	
Smith wins eleven-nine, 11:9	
One game each	
First game (Second) (Third)	
Smith Leads, 2 games to 1	
Match to Smith, 3 games to 1	

Terms	Usage environment
Table moved	In the process of hitting the ball, the body of a player or anything he (she) wears contacts the table making the position of the table moved, which will be penalized one point
Fault service	The ball does not first touch the table of the serving side and does not pass over the net, or does not touch the opponent's table after touching the table of the serving side. This will add one point to the opponent directly
Wrong order Wrong ends	Once a wrong order of serving and receiving or ends is found, the game should be suspended immediately, and continue the game after correction
Penalize one point	A player who violates some provisions in the game will be penalized one point
Best of 5 games	Winning three games (of five)
Best of 7 games	Winning four games (of seven)
Again	Players even up again
Deciding game	The game decides winning or losing
Game point	The point decides the result of a game